PROMPT AND UTTER DESTRUCTION

PROMPT AND UTTER
DESTRUCTION

Truman and the Use of Atomic Bombs against Japan

Third Edition

J. SAMUEL WALKER

The University of North Carolina Press *Chapel Hill*

MIX
Paper from
responsible sources
FSC
www.fsc.org   FSC® C013483

© 2016 The University of North Carolina Press
All rights reserved

Designed and set in Espinosa Nova and Gotham types by Rebecca Evans.
Manufactured in the United States of America. The University of North Carolina Press
has been a member of the Green Press Initiative since 2003.

Cover illustrations: mushroom cloud from test explosion of atomic bomb, Alamogordo,
N.Mex., July 16, 1945, Los Alamos Scientific Laboratory, courtesy Harry S. Truman
Library; view of Hiroshima after the bomb, U.S. Army photo, 1945, Library of Congress.

ISBN 978-1-4696-2897-4 (pbk: alk. paper)
ISBN 978-1-4696-2898-1 (ebook)

The Library of Congress has cataloged the original edition as follows:
Walker, J. Samuel.
Prompt and utter destruction : Truman and the use of atomic bombs against Japan /
by J. Samuel Walker.
p. cm.
Includes bibliographical references and index.
1. World War, 1939–1945—United States. 2. World War, 1939– 1945—Japan. 3. Atomic
bomb. 4. United States—Foreign relations—1945-1953. 5. Truman, Harry S., 1884-1972.
I. Title.
d767.25.h6w355 1997   940.54′25—dc21 96-52038
cip ISBN 0-8078-5607-x (alk. paper)

*This book is dedicated
with love to my children,*
MARY BETH AND DAN

CONTENTS

FIGURES

PREFACE TO THE THIRD EDITION

The use of atomic bombs against Japan in 1945 is, in terms of longevity and intensity, the most controversial issue in all of American history. The central question is: Was the bomb necessary to force a prompt Japanese surrender and end World War II in the Pacific on terms that were acceptable to the United States? The range of opinion on this question is very wide. On one pole, some scholars insist that the bomb was absolutely necessary to win the war without an enormously costly invasion of Japan. At the opposite pole, other scholars condemn the use of the bomb as militarily unnecessary, and some label it a war crime. The debate over this issue has raged for more than five decades, and it has been remarkable for its displays of rancor and intolerance.

Since the original edition of this book appeared in 1997, I have experienced indications of ill will over my views from a few scholars that were both astonishing and amusing. One refused to shake my hand and then, oddly enough, wiped his hand on his trousers. Another ostentatiously turned his back on me. Another pointedly asked me on several occasions if my writings on the bomb were my own work, which made me wonder if this individual routinely impugns the integrity of those with whom she disagrees. Those examples of closed-minded pomposity are exceptional even by the low standards of civility on this issue, but they are consistent with the unyielding dogma that too often has driven the debate. Most scholars and students, however, have responded much more favorably to my book. The feedback I have received from reviewers and other readers across the interpretive spectrum, with the exception of those who stand at the poles of the debate, has been very gratifying.

I have gained great satisfaction from the fact that scores of college professors and secondary school teachers have assigned the book to their classes. Many have told me that it inspires thoughtful, often intense, discussion and helps students to understand the limits of historical knowledge and the passions of historical debate. I am also keenly aware, of course, that some, perhaps most, students appreciate the book not so much for the power of its ideas as for the brevity of its presentation. My goal in this edition, as in the first two, was to keep the book short as well as current with the latest scholarship.

The revisions I have made in this edition draw on scholarly work that has appeared since the second edition was published in 2004. Several scholars have made important contributions to our understanding of President Harry S. Truman's decision to use the bomb and the end of World War II, both from Japanese and American perspectives. The controversy continues, but recent research on the subject has enriched our knowledge of a topic that a poll of journalists ranked in 1999 as the top news story of the twentieth century. It has also inflicted severe if not fatal damage on the claims of writers who make their stands at the far poles of the debate.

University Park, Maryland
June 2015

PREFACE TO THE ORIGINAL EDITION

This book is a labor of love. The question of why President Truman used atomic bombs against Japan has intrigued me since I was an undergraduate history major. Indeed, it was the first issue in which the competing arguments of different scholars caught my interest, in contrast to other historiographical debates that left me befuddled and rather resentful that historians could not make up their minds and agree on revealed truth. When I attended graduate school in history, my understanding of the subjectivity of "truth" in historical interpretation and the reasons for historiographical controversy increased, as did my interest in a wide range of historical topics. At the same time, my interest in the debate over the use of the atomic bomb waned. Even though my field of specialization in graduate school was American diplomatic history, my own research focused on other matters. I thought the work of several scholars who published pathbreaking books and articles in the 1970s had largely resolved the key questions surrounding the use of the bomb.

My thinking turned out to be badly mistaken. New sources opened and new books and articles appeared with fresh things to say about Truman and the bomb. By the time of the fortieth anniversary of Hiroshima in 1985, there was an outpouring of scholarship, much of it very good, on the events leading to the use of the bomb. My own interest in the subject waxed. I decided to catch up on the secondary literature on the subject and try to figure out what we knew and did not know about Truman's decision in light of the new work. The result of my efforts was a historiographical article that attempted to trace the debate and make judgments about where scholars stood on the core issue that divided specialists: was the bomb militarily necessary or was it used primarily for political/diplomatic reasons that had more to do with impressing the Soviets than winning the war against Japan?

The article appeared in the Winter 1990 issue of the journal *Diplomatic History* under the title "The Decision to Use the Bomb: A Historiographical Update." It received more attention than most scholarly articles, at least ones that I had published, and elicited a few spirited reactions from other scholars. But, like most scholarly articles, it was not material that won attention in the national media. I regarded myself as well acquainted with the historical literature on the subject, but at that point, despite the complaints of some historians who thought that I had sided with one position or the other, I had not sorted out my own views of why Truman opted for the bomb.

In the spring of 1995, to my surprise and sometimes to my consternation, the article suddenly hit the mainstream of the popular media—or, to be more accurate, small portions of it did. As the fiftieth anniversary of Hiroshima approached and a major controversy erupted over the plans of the Smithsonian Institution to mount an exhibit on the use of the bomb, the article was widely quoted in dozens of newspaper and magazine articles. On occasion it was quoted accurately. More often it was quoted selectively to prove whatever point the author might wish to make. Through the wonders of software reference systems, writers were able to quote small segments of the article without having to read it.

I received many phone calls from reporters, some of whom were very well informed and very well acquainted with the history of Truman's decision and others who were simply looking for a quote to plug into a story. Some thought I was a revisionist; some thought I was a traditionalist. Some understood that I might not fit neatly into any category; others did not. I hesitated to introduce them to a category that many historians call "postrevisionism," partly because they generally would not have been interested but mostly because I'm not sure myself what that term means. During the months that the question of the bomb's use was making front-page headlines, I also received calls from reporters who were doing stories about the stories being written. I was interviewed on camera and appeared in what turned out to be, in my not unbiased opinion, the best documentary ever made on Truman's decision, the prizewinning ABC News production "Hiroshima: Why the Bomb Was Dropped."

All of this was a flattering, at times exhilarating, and always interesting experience. It was also an unsettling experience. The media attention that suddenly came my way was troubling in part because I was almost invariably identified as the historian of the United States Nuclear Regulatory Commission. That was true enough; my full-time job was (and is) with the NRC, where my primary responsibility is to write a scholarly history of the regulation of commercial nuclear power in the United States. I tried to explain to reporters but apparently failed to convey with sufficient clarity that my work at the NRC does not include research and writing about nuclear weapons. My work on the use of the atomic bomb in 1945 was, and is, an avocation that I conduct on my own time. It is an extension of my interest in the subject of Truman's decision to drop atomic bombs that goes back to my undergraduate days. I wish to state as clearly as I can to try to avoid any further confusion on this matter: this book was not written as a part of my duties as historian of the NRC. It was researched and written entirely on my own time. It represents my own views, based on my reading of primary and secondary sources. It does not in any way represent a position of the NRC.

The attention that my work on Truman's decision received was also unsettling in part because reporters wanted to know why *I* thought the bomb was dropped; they were not particularly interested in a recitation about historiography. Their questions forced me to think more about my own views of why Truman used the bomb than I had done previously and to reach my own conclusions about one of the monumental decisions in American history. This book presents those conclusions as clearly and succinctly as I can. I think I have something new to say, even decades after I decided that scholars had covered the topic so thoroughly that it was historiographically over the hill.

I am personally and intellectually indebted to many friends and scholars who assisted me in the research and writing of this book. Archivists in several institutions were enormously helpful in guiding me to the relevant records and sharing their knowledge about Truman's decision. I am particularly grateful to Ray Geselbracht, Sam Rushay, Liz Safly, Randy Sowell, and Pauline Testerman of the Harry S. Truman Library; Bob Coren, Wil Mahoney, and Mike McReynolds of the National Archives; Tom Camden and Marti Gansz of the George C. Marshall Research

Library; and David Wigdor of the Library of Congress. I am also grateful to the Harry S. Truman Library Institute, which provided a grant for research in the Truman papers and other collections at the library.

A number of friends shared thoughtful opinions, unpublished manuscripts, or copies of documents with me. I am very much indebted to Bart Bernstein for offering encouragement and his vast knowledge of Truman's decision and to Larry Kaplan for providing the dual perspective of not only a scholar but also a veteran who was scheduled to participate in the invasion of Japan. Allan Winkler supplied some important and unusually obscure information at a critical juncture. Elizabeth Sams, coproducer of the ABC documentary "Hiroshima," caused me to revise my stereotypes of filmmakers and, by asking well-informed and thoughtful questions, forced me to articulate my own views on why Truman dropped the bomb.

Other friends and scholars went even further by reading and commenting on draft chapters of this book. Roger Anders provided expertise and attention to detail that saved me from some potentially embarrassing errors. Bill Lanouette offered much encouragement and a journalist's eye for awkward phrases and unclear constructions. Bob Newman and Sadao Asada shared their deep knowledge of the subject. Even when they took issue with my conclusions, they did so in a constructive and supportive way. Wayne Cole, even after his retirement, continues to act as a valued adviser and friendly critic of my work, just as he did many years ago as my dissertation director. Now, as then, he contested some of my conclusions in the best tradition of scholarly investigation and inquiry. Mel Leffler agreed with my conclusions but still raised probing questions about practically every statement I made. I hate it when he does that; but I benefited greatly. I am deeply grateful to all.

I am particularly indebted to my family, whose interest in Truman's decision was perhaps less passionate then mine, for their understanding and tolerance. My wife Pat's support for this project was vital, especially at times when I hit a wall. My daughter Mary Beth shared the computer without complaint and occasionally allowed me to drive "her" car to the copy center. Since this book was written mostly during winter months, my son Dan did not have to unduly sacrifice the benefit of my expertise on the golf course. But he gladly would have done so, and in fact has been known to thrive without it.

University Park, Maryland
October 1996

PROMPT AND UTTER DESTRUCTION

1

A Categorical Choice?

Despite an expression that suggested fatigue and strain, President Harry S. Truman strode briskly into the meeting he had ordered with his most trusted advisers. It was held in July 1945 during the Potsdam Conference, at which Truman was deliberating with British Prime Minister Winston S. Churchill and Soviet Premier Joseph Stalin over the end of World War II in the Pacific and the shape of the postwar world. The president told his advisers that he sought their guidance in order to make a decision about what to do with a new weapon—the atomic bomb. The first test explosion of the weapon had recently taken place in the New Mexico desert, and Truman had described it in his diary as the "most terrible thing ever discovered."[1] He wanted his advisers to consider carefully the need for using the bomb against Japan and to spell out the options available to him.

The president, dapper as always in a double-breasted suit with a care-fully folded handkerchief and two-color wing tips, nodded to Secretary of War Henry L. Stimson to open the discussion. Stimson had headed the War Department since Franklin D. Roosevelt had appointed him in 1940, and given that he was the cabinet member directly responsible for winning the war, his demanding duties had taken a toll. At age 78, his health was failing, but he remained as active as possible. Stimson commanded the respect of his colleagues and deputies, even if they did not always agree with him, in part because he was an embodiment of integrity and dignity. His knowledge of the atomic bomb exceeded that of any other cabinet official, and he had reflected deeply on its implications for American military and diplomatic policies.

The successful test of the bomb, Stimson pointed out at the meeting, gave the United States an important addition to its arsenal for achieving both diplomatic and military objectives. "The bomb as a merely probable weapon [was] a weak reed on which to rely," he observed, "but the bomb as a colossal reality [is] very different." Stimson went on to recommend that the bomb be used against Japan in order to end the war as soon as possible and avoid the huge numbers of American casualties that an invasion would incur. An assault on the Japanese islands, he told the president, "might be expected to cost over a million casualties to American forces alone."[2]

The president then called on General George C. Marshall, the U.S. Army chief of staff, the highest post that a professional soldier could attain. Marshall, reserved, taciturn, and levelheaded, personified the ideal of a career military officer. He had earned the admiration of both superiors and subordi-nates for his fairness, frankness, and thoughtful consideration of the options available when making policy decisions. George F. Kennan, who worked for Marshall after the general became Truman's secretary of state in 1947,

FIGURE 1 General George C. Marshall and Secretary of War Henry L. Stimson confer in Marshall's office, January 1942. (The George C. Marshall Research Library, Lexington, Virginia)

recalled "his indifference to the whims and moods of public opinion" and his discomfort with the political aspects of his job.[3]

Marshall agreed with the views that Stimson expressed on the question of the use of the atomic bomb. He was skeptical that attacking Japanese cities with conventional weapons would end the war, "despite what generals with cigars in their mouths had to say about bombing the Japanese into submission." Marshall pointedly reminded the president and the others at the meeting that in a massive raid on Tokyo in March 1945, "we killed 100,000 Japanese . . . but it didn't mean a thing insofar as actually beating the Japanese." He also revealed that "Churchill estimated that we would sustain 500,000 casualties" in an invasion. Therefore, the use of atomic bombs seemed to be the best way to avoid such shocking numbers of dead, wounded, and missing Americans.[4]

Truman turned next to James F. Byrnes, who recently had assumed the post of secretary of state. Byrnes had served in the U.S. Senate, where he and Truman had been colleagues, and more recently as a powerful and intimate adviser to President Roosevelt. He had wielded so much authority that he had earned the title "assistant president." When Roosevelt had decided to replace Vice President Henry A. Wallace with a new running mate at the 1944 Democratic convention, many observers, including Byrnes himself, thought

Byrnes deserved the nomination. In contrast to Marshall, Byrnes thought primarily and instinctively in political terms when assessing policy issues.

Charming, bright, and capable, he was an operator, a doer, and at times a sleight-of-hand artist. Truman described him in his diary as "my able and conniving Secretary of State." At the time of Potsdam, Byrnes enjoyed easier access to and greater influence on the president than any other adviser. Although he approached the question of using the atomic bomb from a perspective different from that of Stimson and Marshall, he reached the same conclusion. The bomb was needed, he suggested, to spare "the lives of hundreds of thousands of American soldiers." He also argued that by shortening the war, it would save "the lives of hundreds of thousands of Japanese boys and millions more of [the] Japanese people."⁵

Truman quickly made it clear that he agreed with his advisers. He declared that the two available atomic bombs should be dropped on Japanese cities because "an invasion would cost at a minimum one quarter of a million casualties, and might cost as much as a million, on the American side alone." The president added that "a quarter of a million of the flower of our young manhood was worth a couple of Japanese cities."⁶ Truman's statement brought the meeting to a close; none of the cabinet members or military officials present expressed a dissenting view. The choice between using the bomb and facing the grim prospect of a bloody invasion of Japan seemed obvious.

The meeting described above never took place. The quotations are authentic, but the context is not. With the exception of two notations from Truman's diary, the statements quoted were made after the war to explain why the bomb was dropped. Those statements and many others expressing the same views created a widely held myth about the decision to use atomic bombs against Japan—the belief that Truman had to choose between, on the one hand, authorizing attacks on Japanese cities with atomic bombs or, on the other hand, ordering an invasion.

Fifty years after World War II ended, an overwhelming majority of Americans who were alive at the time agreed with the decision to use atomic weapons against Japan in 1945, presumably because of the prevailing myth that the only alternative was an invasion. A 1995 Gallup survey showed that Americans between the ages of 50 and 64 approved the action by a margin of 72 percent to 24 percent; Americans aged 65 and older approved it by an even wider margin, 80 percent to 13 percent. A poll conducted 20 years later by the Pew Research Center produced similar, but somewhat more equivocal, results. It showed that 56 percent of Americans believed the use of atomic bombs was "justified," while 34 percent thought it was "not justified." Like the earlier Gallup poll, the Pew survey highlighted a sharp generational gap. Seventy percent of the respondents who were 65 or older supported the use of the bomb, while only 47 percent of those between the ages of 18 and 29 agreed with them.[7]

Despite the perception that still prevails among a majority of Americans and is especially strong among older citizens, Truman never faced a categorical choice between the bomb and an invasion that would cost hundreds of thousands of American lives. A rich abundance of historical evidence makes clear that the popular view about the use of the bomb vastly oversimplifies the situation in the summer of 1945 as the Truman administration weighed its options for ending the Pacific war. The majority opinion is unsound for the following reasons: (1) there were other options available for ending the war within a reasonably short time without the bomb and without an invasion; (2) Truman and his key advisers believed Japan was so weak that the war could end before an invasion began—that is, they did not regard an invasion as inevitable; and (3) even in the worst case, if an invasion of Japan proved to be necessary, military planners in the summer of 1945 projected the number of American lives lost at far fewer than the hundreds of thousands that Truman and his advisers claimed after the war.

If the bomb was not required to end the war within a short time, avoid a certain invasion of Japan, or save hundreds of thousands of American lives, two fundamental questions have to be addressed: (1) was the use of the bomb necessary at all, and (2) if so, what exactly did it accomplish? Historically sound conclusions can be reached only by examining conditions and decision making in the United States and Japan in the summer of 1945 and by recognizing that the considerations that led to Hiroshima were much more complex and much less clear-cut than the conventional view suggests. It is equally essential to realize that some important questions about the use of the bomb will never be answered in a definitive or unassailable way because they are matters of speculation, assumption, or uncertainty rather than matters of conclusive evidence.

2

The Most Terrible Weapon Ever Known

One reason for the prevalence and tenacity of popular misconceptions about the use of the bomb is the mythology that has surrounded the central figure in the decision, President Truman. Truman won greater affection and esteem from the American people after his presidency, and especially after his death, than he ever achieved when he occupied the White House. In the public image of his performance as president that gradually emerged after he left office, he was honest, forthright, confident, and decisive (guided by the sign on his desk, "The Buck Stops Here"). In popular perceptions, he was, despite his limited formal education and executive experience, instinctively right in his policy judgments, using down-to-earth common sense to address complicated issues. This image of Truman, while not totally inaccurate, is deceptively incomplete. His honesty was often tempered by political considerations. His bluntness could be indiscreet or needlessly offensive. His decisiveness could lead to superficial or impulsive judgments. And his confidence was often a show that disguised insecurity and self-doubt. Historian Alonzo L. Hamby, the most perceptive analyst of Truman's personality, has described him as loyal, considerate, thoughtful, and courageous, and at the same time petty, vindictive, thin-skinned, and suspicious. "It will not do to ask which was the real Harry Truman," Hamby has observed. "Both were the real Harry Truman."[1] Truman had his faults as well as his admirable qualities, and it is essential to recognize both. The myths about him have not only robbed him of a portion of his humanity by placing him on a pedestal but also helped to obscure the complexity of the considerations that led to Hiroshima.

When Truman became president after Roosevelt's death on April 12, 1945, he was very unsure of himself and his abilities. "Boys, if you ever pray, pray for me now," he remarked to a group of reporters the day after he was sworn into office. "When they told me yesterday what had happened, I felt like the moon, the stars, and all the planets had fallen on me."[2] Truman's doubts about himself were reflected, indeed magnified, in the views of other government officials and the American public. The president was, through no fault of his own, ill-informed and poorly prepared for the responsibilities he assumed. Roosevelt had not confided in him or attempted to explain his positions on key policy questions.

To make matters worse, Truman became president at a time when he faced a series of extraordinarily difficult problems. In April 1945 the war in Europe was ending, but the war in the Pacific still had to be won. Americans were growing weary of the war and the sacrifices it demanded.

Tensions with the Soviet Union were increasing over seemingly intractable issues. The reconversion to a peacetime economy required tough decisions that could not be put off for long. Truman's primary challenge on the economic front was to keep the United States from plunging back into depression and calming pervasive fears that the end of the war would mean the end of prosperity.

Those problems would have severely tried the abilities of any president, but Truman's difficulties were compounded by confronting them suddenly without adequate preparation. It is little wonder, therefore, that he relied heavily on his predecessor's advisers to provide information and guidance on what Roosevelt's policies and intentions had been. He was committed to carrying out Roosevelt's legacy, but he was often uncertain about what the legacy was, especially in the critical area of foreign affairs. In the early months of his presidency, Truman vacillated over whose recommendations to accept when he received conflicting advice from Roosevelt's appointees. In those cases, he was far from being the decisive leader of legend. Rather, he was inclined to indicate his support for the position of whomever he was talking to at a given moment. Henry Wallace, who after his involuntary departure from the post of vice president had become secretary of commerce, was asked by newspaper columnist Marquis Childs in October 1945 how he was getting along with Truman. Wallace replied that their relationship "had been the most friendly; that the President had cooperated with me in everything I had wanted." Childs commented: "Well, that is one of the great difficulties with the President; he does that way with everyone."[3] Truman's expressions of agreement "with everyone" enabled him to avoid unpleasant confrontations and difficult choices; it also gave greater influence on policy decisions to whichever of his advisers saw him most often or at the most opportune times.

Although Truman began his presidency in the dark about many of his predecessor's policies and commitments, one issue on which Roosevelt's legacy seemed clear was his philosophy for fighting the war. The fundamental military strategy that Roosevelt adopted was to achieve complete victory at the lowest cost in American lives. To the extent possible, the United States would use its industrial might and technological prowess to reduce the number of casualties it would suffer on battlefronts. Roosevelt made this point to a radio audience on November 2, 1944: "In winning this war there is just one sure way to guarantee the minimum of casualties—by seeing to it that, in every action, we have overwhelming material superiority."[4] And, as his biographer James MacGregor Burns suggested, Roosevelt's strategy was extremely successful. "Compared with Soviet, German, and even British losses," Burns wrote, "and considering the range and intensity of the effort and skilled and fanatical resistance of the enemy, American casualties in World War II were remarkably light."[5] Truman inherited from Roosevelt the strategy of keeping American losses to a minimum, and he was committed to carrying it out for the remainder of the war.

In addition to his determination to fulfill Roosevelt's legacy, Truman sought to curtail American casualties as much as possible because of his own combat experience. As an artillery captain during World War I, he had faced hostile fire, endured forced marches, slogged through mud, slept under bushes, and seen American soldiers killed by the enemy. He performed admirably and courageously, and he learned firsthand about the fear, fatigue, and camaraderie of combat. Truman confided to his fiancée Bess Wallace the depth of his feelings about the loss of a comrade when one of his men died while waiting to be shipped home from France. "I have been rather sorrowful the last day or so. My Battery clerk died in the hospital from appendicitis," he wrote on January 26, 1919. "I know exactly how it would feel to lose a son. . . . When the letter came from the hospital informing me of his death I acted like a real baby. . . . I certainly hope I don't lose another man until we are mustered out."[6] Truman therefore not only sympathized with Roosevelt's strategy of winning the war at the lowest possible cost in American casualties on a policy level; he empathized with it on a personal level.

The development of the atomic bomb was the most dramatic example of how the Roosevelt and Truman administrations devoted their scientific, engineering, and industrial assets to a project that they hoped would help win the war at the earliest possible time. It proved to be literally an earthshaking application of the American strategy of depending on industry and technology to reduce combat losses. Although other nations sponsored modest nuclear research programs, the United States was the only belligerent that could spare the human talent and industrial resources required to build an atomic bomb in time to use it during the war.

After October 1941, when Roosevelt authorized a major effort to explore the feasibility of an atomic bomb, it was an undertaking of monumental proportions. The initial impetus for the project came from the fear that Nazi Germany, home of many leading nuclear physicists, would build an atomic bomb. A letter from Albert Einstein first alerted

Roosevelt to this danger. Scientists had greatly increased their understanding of nuclear physics during the 1930s, but many vital questions remained to be answered about whether the enormous energy in the nucleus of an atom could be released in an explosive of unprecedented magnitude.

Roosevelt was concerned that German scientists would find answers to those questions first. The American project was assigned to the U.S. Army Corps of Engineers; it soon came to be called the Manhattan Project because a new "engineer district" created to build the bomb was originally headquartered in New York. Under the direction of General Leslie R. Groves, a demanding, blunt, impatient, and energetic officer with a well-deserved reputation for getting things done, the Manhattan Project set out to address a bewildering variety of scientific and engineering uncertainties.

The scientific breakthrough for the Manhattan Project, and for the future of nuclear energy, occurred in December 1942 in a squash court beneath a grandstand at the football field of the University of Chicago. A team of scientists led by Enrico Fermi, a Nobel Prize–winning physicist who had fled his native Italy, produced the first self-sustaining nuclear chain reaction. Neutrons released by the fission of the nuclei of uranium atoms freed other neutrons to keep the reaction going. This proved conclusively that an atomic bomb many times more powerful than conventional explosives was possible. Fermi and his colleagues had anticipated those results, but it was still a large step from the experimental knowledge that a nuclear weapon could be built to the development of an actual bomb.

To design a workable bomb, Groves needed scientific talent that could address outstanding issues, perform tests, and reach conclusions about how to transform theory into a weapon of war. He asked J. Robert Oppenheimer, a brilliant and charismatic theoretical physicist from the University of California at Berkeley, to lead the scientific effort. Oppenheimer was in many ways the polar opposite of Groves—philosophical, reflective, mystical, and eclectic in his wide-ranging interests. Even in appearance the gaunt, chain-smoking Oppenheimer contrasted with the corpulent, chocolate-munching Groves. But they worked together well, and Oppenheimer was instrumental in recruiting a cadre of top scientists to collaborate on building an atomic bomb.[7]

Once it was proven that a nuclear chain reaction would take place under the right conditions, the Manhattan Project focused on two principal tasks. One was the design of a bomb; the other was the production of fuel to make it work. To determine how to fabricate an atomic bomb, a group of gifted scientists enlisted and led by Oppenheimer assembled at the hastily built community of Los Alamos, New Mexico, an isolated site over 7,000 feet high on a mesa near Santa Fe. Meanwhile, another boomtown sprang up in Tennessee, then called the Clinton Engineer Works and later renamed Oak Ridge, to deal with the equally difficult challenge of making nuclear fuel. The problem was that uranium 235—the isotope that is "fissionable," or usable for nuclear fuel—is extremely rare, constituting only about 0.7 percent of naturally occurring uranium. To isolate enough uranium 235 for a bomb, it had to be separated from the more plentiful uranium 238. There were four approaches that scientists thought might be used to isolate sufficient quantities of uranium 235, but none was certain and none was easy. An alternative fuel for a bomb was plutonium, an artificially made element that had been discovered only in early 1941 in the form of a microscopic speck. Scientists calculated that several pounds of plutonium would be needed for a bomb, and they could offer no guarantee that, even if such a large quantity could be produced, it would be suitable for creating an atomic explosion.

Groves was committed to moving ahead on atomic research and production as quickly as possible; the United States did not learn until the European war was almost ended that the Germans had made little progress toward building an atomic bomb. Unrestrained by fiscal considerations and racing to beat the Nazis, he pushed ahead by constructing huge production facilities without first testing approaches for isolating uranium 235 in pilot plants. He focused on two methods for separating uranium 235 by taking advantage of the slightly greater atomic weight of uranium 238—an electromagnetic process and gaseous diffusion. Groves also built an immense complex along the Columbia River, the Hanford Engineer Works, in lightly populated eastern Washington. It was a collection of nuclear reactors to produce plutonium and other plants equipped to extract it chemically from other elements. During 1943 and 1944, the Manhattan Project sponsored research on bomb designs at Los Alamos, attempts at isolating uranium 235 at Oak Ridge, construction of reactors at Hanford, and other vital activities at dozens of laboratories and industrial sites. It employed tens of thousands of people, few of whom had any idea what they were working on.

After experimentation and deliberation, the scientists designing the bomb concluded that there were two promising approaches. The simpler one would shoot together two subcritical masses of uranium 235 to create a "critical mass" and set off a chain reaction. This gun-type design seemed almost certain to work; the key was to produce enough uranium 235. Scientists discovered that the same design was not suitable with plutonium. Therefore they turned to a problematical and intricate system of "implosion," in which small amounts of plutonium would be compressed together by symmetrical shockwaves to form a critical mass. The prospects for this design were less certain. After many false starts, unpleasant surprises, and modified plans, the Manhattan Project achieved substantial progress. Groves told President Roosevelt in December 1944 that one gun-type bomb fueled by uranium 235 would be ready by August 1, 1945, and that it could be used without a field test. The plutonium bomb would have to be tested, but Groves informed the president that the first implosion weapon would be completed by July 1945 and, if it worked, several more would be available over the following few months.[8]

When Truman became president, he knew virtually nothing about the Manhattan Project. While still a member of the Senate and serving as chairman of the Special Committee to Investigate the National Defense Program, he had learned of a massive and highly secret effort to build a new weapon, but he did not receive any details. Roosevelt had not revealed any information to Truman during his brief tenure as vice president. On the day Truman was sworn into the presidency, Stimson told him that he needed to brief him about "a most urgent matter," which left the president "puzzled." Within a short time, Truman found out from Byrnes that the subject of Stimson's request was a bomb that "might be so powerful as to be potentially capable of wiping out entire cities and killing people on an unprecedented scale."[9]

In a meeting on April 25, 1945, Stimson confirmed and elaborated on the information that Byrnes had provided the president. Stimson handed Truman a memorandum that began with a sobering statement: "Within four months we shall in all probability have completed the most terrible weapon ever known in human history, one bomb of which could destroy a whole city." The secretary of war went on to warn the president that the existence of such a weapon would create profound problems because the United States would not be able to maintain a monopoly on the technology. Further, the issue of sharing information about the atomic bomb would become "a primary question of our foreign relations." Handled unwisely, atomic weapons could mean the end of civilization, but handled skillfully, wrote Stimson, "we would have the opportunity to bring the world into a pattern in which the peace of the world and our civilization can be saved."[10]

Truman listened attentively to Stimson's briefing, and after they had talked alone for a time, Groves, who had been waiting in another room, joined the meeting. He gave the president a lengthy memorandum about the origins, development, and status of the Manhattan Project. Truman was less interested in or capable of understanding the technical details and, to Groves's exasperation, was not inclined to read the paper carefully. Groves told him the same thing he had reported to Roosevelt four months earlier—that the uranium 235 bomb would be ready around August 1 and would not need a test before use in combat. The plutonium bomb would be ready for a test shot early in July. It was not clear how much Truman absorbed or remembered of the information that Stimson and Groves offered about the Manhattan Project. But he undoubtedly grasped the basic message about the bomb's potential for providing unprecedented and unparalleled explosive power. The president agreed to Stimson's request that a special committee of high-level advisers be established to consider the implications of the new weapon, especially, in light of Stimson's concerns, for the postwar era.

Within a few days, Stimson formed the committee, which he called the "Interim Committee," and received Truman's approval of the membership. Stimson served as chairman, with his aide George L. Harrison as his alternate. The other members were William L. Clayton, assistant secretary of state; Ralph A. Bard, undersecretary of the navy; Karl T. Compton, president of the Massachusetts Institute of Technology; Vannevar Bush, director of the Office of Scientific Research and Development and the top scientific administrator of the Manhattan Project; James B. Conant, president of Harvard University and Bush's right-hand man; and James F. Byrnes, whom Truman had designated but not yet announced as his secretary of state. Byrnes, at the recommendation of Stimson, was Truman's personal representative on the committee. In addition, Marshall, Groves, Oppenheimer, and a few others attended at least some of the Interim Committee's meetings by invitation.

In five meetings between May 9 and June 1, 1945, the members of the committee discussed a broad range of topics. They did not, however, deliberate over the issue of whether Japan should be attacked with the new weapon; they assumed that once the bomb was ready it would be used. In the limited time that the Interim Committee devoted to the impact of the bomb on the war against Japan, the members considered not whether it should be dropped but the most advantageous way to demonstrate its power and help force a Japanese surrender. They reached agreement that the bomb should be employed without any advance warning; the objective would be "to make a profound psychological impression on as many of the inhabitants as possible." Stimson accepted Conant's suggestion "that the most desirable target would be a vital war plant employing a large number of workers and closely surrounded by workers' houses."[11] The purpose was to impede the Japanese capacity for making war and to shock the Japanese people and government officials with the fearful power and terrifying visual effects of an atomic explosion. The committee realized that the target area it recommended would include not only factory workers but also their families who lived in nearby houses. A few days after the committee reached those conclusions, Stimson passed them along to Truman.

The Interim Committee spent much more time on the issue that had led to its creation, the possible effects of the bomb on international politics in the postwar era. The focus of this discussion was the most important and most perplexing foreign policy problem that faced the United States—its relations with the Soviet Union. The wartime alliance between the United States and Britain on the one hand and the Soviet Union on the other had always been an awkward and uneasy coalition that was held together principally by their struggle against a common enemy, Nazi Germany. As the war in Europe ground to a close in the spring of 1945, tensions between the allies increased. One pivotal matter of dispute was the future of Poland. During the Yalta Conference in February 1945, Roosevelt, Churchill, and Stalin had reached an agreement on Poland that was purposely vague and, as a result, subject to different interpretations. Stalin was convinced, with good reason, that Roosevelt had ceded him a sphere of interest over a nation that the Soviets considered vital to their security. Roosevelt hoped that Stalin would exercise his dominance in a way that was not heavy-handed and would allow the Poles a semblance of independence. Soviet behavior in Poland turned out to be so incompatible with Roosevelt's view of the understandings at Yalta that he strongly protested to Stalin. But he remained hopeful that the conflict would be resolved.

When Truman took office, he was outraged by Soviet conduct in Poland. Poorly informed about the ambiguity of the Yalta agreement and told by several of Roosevelt's advisers that the Soviets were brazenly violating their promises, he quickly decided to vent his indignation. When Soviet Foreign Minister Vyacheslav Molotov visited Truman on April 23, less than two weeks after Roosevelt's death, the president gave him a stern lecture and brusquely demanded that the Soviets carry out the Yalta accords on Poland. Truman's scolding of Molotov disturbed Stimson and others who regarded it as inappropriate and unnecessarily confrontational. The president's bluntness and his desire to be decisive prevailed over the need for carefully considered responses to a delicate situation.

Truman did not want a rupture in U.S.-Soviet relations, in part because he was committed to Roosevelt's policy of trying to get along with Stalin and in part because he wished to make certain that the Soviet Union would enter the war against Japan. The Soviets and Japanese had signed a nonaggression pact in April 1941, and both had observed the agreement during the war because it served their interests to do so. One of Roosevelt's most important goals and major achievements at Yalta was to secure Stalin's assent to enter the Asian war within three months after victory in Europe. The United States anticipated that a Soviet invasion of Manchuria would tie down Japanese troops and prevent them from being transferred across the Sea of Japan to help defend the homeland from an American invasion.

A short time after his tense session with Molotov, Truman sought to ease U.S.-Soviet divisions by sending former Roosevelt confidant Harry Hopkins to confer with Stalin. In his talks with Hopkins, Stalin reaffirmed his intention to join the war against Japan. The meetings also produced an acceptable formula to settle the dispute over Poland.

It was in this context that the Interim Committee weighed the impact of the atomic bomb on U.S.-Soviet relations. The central importance of the issue was apparent. As the minutes of a meeting on May 31 noted: "In considering the problem of controls and international collaboration the question of paramount concern was the attitude of Russia." American policymakers recognized that relations between the United States and the Soviet Union were the key to postwar peace. They were much less certain about the chances for or the means of achieving postwar harmony without sacrificing other important U.S. goals. The prospects for American possession and use of the atomic bomb introduced a new variable to the already difficult problem of evaluating the best way to deal with the Soviet Union. The ideological conflicts and the divergent wartime objectives of the two nations, along with the political and economic chaos that the war created in Europe, made the growth of U.S.-Soviet tensions inevitable. The question that the Interim Committee faced, in attempting to assess how the atomic bomb would affect U.S.-Soviet relations, was whether the United States should attempt to ease differences and allay Soviet suspicions or whether it should try to advance American objectives by intimidating the Soviets.

The committee discussed two ways to approach this question. One was to offer general information to Stalin about the American effort to build the bomb in hopes that it would foster cooperation between the United States and the Soviet Union. The other was to seek to maintain a lead over the Soviets and other nations in hopes that the bomb would give the United States greater leverage in achieving diplomatic objectives, at least for a time. The debate within the committee was settled by Byrnes, the president's personal representative. He objected to providing even general information to Stalin and declared "that the most desirable program would be to push ahead as fast as possible in production and research to make certain that we stay ahead." Byrnes's view "was generally agreed to by all present."[12]

The committee's concurrence with Byrnes reflected his influence and his status as the president's spokesman rather than a solid consensus in favor of his arguments. Although Byrnes expressed support for making "every effort to better our political relations with Russia," he hoped the atomic bomb would increase his clout in dealing with the Soviets.[13] In a meeting with Leo Szilard, a Manhattan Project scientist who urged him to share information with the Soviet Union in order to head off an arms race, he made his position more clear. Szilard was a brilliant physicist who had first recognized the possibility of a nuclear chain reaction that could lead to an atomic explosion. He had persuaded Einstein to write the letter to Roosevelt about the danger of Nazi Germany building a bomb first. He was also a persistent and eccentric gadfly who had been a huge annoyance to Groves throughout the war. He and Byrnes were far removed in background, personality, experience, and perspectives on public issues, and their ideas on how to deal with the bomb were equally distant. According to an article that Szilard published years later, Byrnes responded to his appeal by suggesting that the use of the atomic bomb would impress the Soviets with American power and make them "more manageable" in Eastern Europe.[14]

Truman's view of the potential diplomatic advantages of the atomic bomb was similar to that of Byrnes. He also hoped it would be useful in advancing American objectives. In May 1945, the president insisted on putting off a conference with Stalin and Churchill until mid-July, despite their preference for meeting sooner to resolve outstanding issues. Truman wanted to delay the conference until after the first test of the plutonium bomb, which was then planned for early July. He reasoned that a successful test would improve his bargaining position with the two tough and experienced leaders, whom he would be meeting for the first time.

At the end of May 1945 the looming presence of the atomic bomb was a source of great hope and great uncertainty for the small number of officials who knew about it. They hoped that the new weapon would speed the end of the war with Japan. But there was much about the bomb and its applications that remained in doubt. Although Groves had told Truman on April 25 that a uranium 235 bomb was almost sure to work and would be ready about August 1, the president and his advisers did not accept this assessment on the general's word. They attached great importance to the upcoming test of the plutonium bomb for both military and diplomatic purposes. The long-term implications of the bomb for international politics and especially for U.S.-Soviet relations had already proven to be a complex and divisive issue.

The Interim Committee had pondered many of the key questions raised by the anticipated availability of the bomb. Rather than providing answers to those questions, the committee's deliberations had demonstrated the assumptions, priorities, and inclinations of knowledgeable and thoughtful officials. Although the committee was not a policymaking body and its conclusions were in no way binding, its discussions were harbingers of the considerations that weighed heavily in future decisions about the use of the bomb: the commitment to ending the war with Japan as quickly as possible, the assumption that the bomb would be used when it became available, the willingness to attack civilian targets as a legitimate means of waging war, and the hope that the bomb would help advance American diplomatic objectives, especially in addressing the growing differences with the Soviet Union.

3

The Prospects for Victory, June 1945

On May 8, 1945, less than a month after Truman became president, Germany surrendered to the Allied forces and the war in Europe ended. This was cause for satisfaction and relief in the United States, but jubilation had to wait until Japan surrendered and the global conflict came to a close. Neither soldiers in the field nor policymakers in Washington anticipated that forcing Japan to quit the war would be an easy task. For the first time, the United States would be able to focus its energies and power on the Pacific campaign—as long as it lasted, the war in Europe had received top priority. Nevertheless, the prospects of facing an implacable enemy determined to defend its empire and its homeland were sobering and daunting, even if the Japanese were badly weakened and reeling toward defeat.

In the three and a half years after the Japanese assault on Pearl Harbor, the Pacific war had proven to be a dreadfully savage affair. In the words of historian John W. Dower, it was a "war without mercy," even more brutal and dehumanizing than the European conflict. "As World War Two recedes in time and scholars dig at the formal documents," Dower wrote, "it is easy to forget the visceral emotions and sheer race hate that gripped virtually all participants in the war, at home and overseas."[1]

Americans regarded Japanese with hatred of singular intensity, exceeding even their antipathy toward Germans. One reason was the Japanese bombing of Pearl Harbor, a surprise attack that not only enraged Americans but humiliated them as well. Another reason Americans detested the Japanese with special ferocity was a series of hideous atrocities that the Imperial Army had committed. During the war, Americans knew more about Japanese barbarities than German ones; the horrors of the Holocaust did not become widespread public knowledge until after the Nazi surrender. Americans had been shocked and incensed by the aerial bombing of civilian targets that the Japanese had carried out in their war against China. Those feelings were intensified by the Rape of Nanking in 1937, during which Japanese troops raped, tortured, and killed hundreds of thousands of Chinese noncombatants, and by reports of the rape and murder of nuns in Hong Kong, the mutilation and hanging of Englishmen in Malaya, the beheading of prisoners for sport, and other outrageous acts.

The U.S. government fueled the hatred when it released information about Japanese mistreatment of American prisoners. In April 1943 it announced that the Japanese had executed three American fliers who had participated in bombing Tokyo during a daring raid led by Colonel

Jimmy Doolittle the previous year. The wave of revulsion that followed this report recurred in early 1944 when the government released information about Japanese brutalities during the Bataan Death March of 1942. Tens of thousands of American and Filipino troops were starved, beaten, left for dead, or executed during a grueling march to a prisoner-of-war camp. In May 1945 the War Department released to the public photographs and reports of Japanese executions of American servicemen; one photograph showed a Japanese soldier with a raised sword about to decapitate a kneeling, blindfolded prisoner (later identified as an Australian). The graphic evidence of Japanese atrocities and inhumanity toward prisoners and civilians fed an image of an enemy that was cruel, barbarous, and deserving of annihilation.[2]

In addition to their feelings in reaction to the attack on Pearl Harbor and the perpetration of unspeakable atrocities, Americans felt an especially deep hatred of the Japanese for racial reasons. Racial stereotypes and animosities were a powerful element in the Pacific war. Americans often viewed the Japanese as a subhuman or inhuman race and depicted them as vermin, reptiles, rats, or, most commonly, apes or monkeys. Racially charged epithets such as "yellow rats," "yellow monkeys," or the consensus favorite, "yellow bastards," vividly demonstrated widely held attitudes.

Before the war, most Americans held Japanese military capabilities in contempt. One reason the Pearl Harbor attack came as a shock was the assumption that the Japanese lacked the means and the skill to carry out such a difficult operation. After a series of Japanese victories over American and European forces in the Far East in late 1941 and early 1942, however, the image of the Japanese military was reversed. Instead of contemptible, inept, and subhuman creatures, they became hardened, invincible, and superhuman fighters. "Gone in a flash were the nearsighted, wobbly Japanese flyers of yesterday," wrote Dower of one aspect of the startling transformation in how Americans viewed their enemy. "Now they were men with telescopic vision, and infernally clever to boot."[3] The image of the Japanese superman coexisted with the image of the Japanese primate. Despite the diametrical contrast of those images, they both conveyed the impression that the Japanese differed from Americans or Europeans not only in their race and culture but also in the fundamental nature of their humanity.

For their part, the Japanese viewed Americans with equal hatred based on similarly warped stereotypes. They considered themselves racially superior not only to Westerners but also to other Asians. They disparaged the European colonial powers as weak and spoiled, and they were convinced that Americans were too soft to respond effectively to the Pearl Harbor attack. Those impressions were intensified by Japan's stunning military successes in the months after Pearl Harbor. Japanese contempt for their vanquished foes helped to incite the atrocities that their troops committed.

When the tide turned and American forces advanced across the Pacific in their island campaign, Japanese soldiers and civilians regarded them as brutal monsters who had no regard for human life and who were hell-bent on rape and murder. Thus, the Japanese view of Americans mirrored the American view of Japanese. And in some cases, the actions of Americans mirrored the atrocities of the Imperial Army and gave credibility to the propaganda of the Japanese government. There were enough instances of unarmed Japanese prisoners being shot, lifeboats strafed, and even on occasion civilians abused or killed to kindle Japanese bitterness toward their enemy.

It was under those conditions that the "war without mercy" was fought. For Americans, it was a campaign of amphibious assaults on islands held by Japanese troops who were determined to drive back the invaders or, in the later stages of the war, to inflict heavy casualties even in a lost cause. The patterns of the battles were similar and the results were the same. After American ships and planes bombarded Japanese positions, troops filled landing vessels that took them across reefs to the beaches, though sometimes the boats got stuck or unloaded their heavily weighted passengers in deep water. In the early attacks, the assault troops faced withering fire as they slogged onto the beaches. Casualties for the first waves were inevitably high. Eventually, once the Americans landed enough troops and enough firepower, they managed to overcome Japanese resistance. But achieving their objective was a wretched and terrifying experience for individual soldiers. Journalist and historian William Manchester, who participated in several offensives in the Pacific as a Marine enlisted man, later recalled the faces of his battle-weary comrades: "haggard, with jaws hanging open and the expressionless eyes of men who had left nowhere and were going nowhere."[4]

The places they had left and to which they were going were a progression of obscure islands that were stepping-stones across the Pacific to defeat Japan. The bloody fighting on Guadalcanal, Tarawa, Tinian, Saipan, Iwo Jima, and other outposts confirmed the hatred and reinforced the images that Americans held of the Japanese. With inevitable loss of life among the members of their combat units and harrowing individual risk, they were forced to flush soldiers from caves, pillboxes, and other defenses, endure suicidal banzai attacks, and conquer an enemy that refused to surrender. The Japanese, it seemed, were not only ruthless and brutal but also fanatical in fighting to the death. The unwillingness of Japanese soldiers to surrender in a lost cause reflected in part their samurai code, devotion to the emperor, and belief that death in battle ensured a glorious destination for their spirits. But their refusal to surrender was also motivated by more mundane considerations, particularly their conviction that death was preferable to the treatment they would suffer at the hands of their American captors.

The reluctance of the Japanese to surrender, to the shock of victorious American forces, extended to noncombatants, voluntarily or otherwise. After overcoming stiff resistance on the island of Saipan in July 1944, Americans were horrified by the spectacle of Japanese soldiers shooting civilians, even those carrying children, who attempted to give themselves up to the Marines. Even more traumatic was the sight of hundreds of civilians who joined the remnants of the Japanese army in death by jumping off steep cliffs, sometimes holding children, or blowing themselves up with grenades. The suicides of noncombatants were a consequence of the stories they had been told about the cruelty and bestial behavior of American soldiers.

In the battle for the barren island of Iwo Jima in February 1945, Americans sustained heavy casualties at the hands of the Japanese, who allowed them to land with little resistance but then attacked in force from well-concealed pillboxes and concrete bunkers. The Americans eventually prevailed, but for the first time in the island campaign they suffered more casualties (though not more fatalities) than their foes. The Japanese again held out to the death; more than 18,000 out of a garrison of 21,000 died, and only slightly more than 200 surrendered (the rest were unaccounted for).[5] American forces attained their objective, but at a cost of 6,821 killed and nearly 20,000 wounded. One Marine's comment spoke for the attitudes of his compatriots: "I hope to God that we don't have to go on any more of those screwy islands."[6]

The American successes in the island campaign sealed the fate of the Japanese empire. But if the demise of the so-called Co-Prosperity Sphere became certain, the costs of the victory were still uncertain. The challenge of making the inevitable happen still remained. The conquest of Saipan and the nearby islands of Tinian and Guam, all of which were a part of the Mariana Islands, was a vital turning point for the American war effort in the Pacific. For the first time, it gave the United States the use of airfields that were within striking distance of the Japanese islands for its new B-29 bombers. The B-29 was a major technological advance over the planes available to U.S. flyers in the European war; it could carry a full bomb load for 3,000 miles or more at a considerably faster speed than older heavy bombers. A flight from the Marianas to Japanese cities was long, arduous, and dangerous, but it was possible, and by late 1944, waves of B-29s were attacking targets in the home islands.[7]

Even as the B-29s began bombing raids on Japan, the official American strategy for aerial attacks on enemy cities was rather ill-defined. Long before World War II, it became apparent that developments in aeronautical technology posed a dire threat to the traditional principle of avoiding attacks on civilians or cultural treasures. The Japanese practice of bombing cities during its war with China and Nazi air raids against noncombatants during the Spanish Civil War had aroused outraged protests, including Picasso's dramatic painting *Guernica*. For a time after the European war broke out, both Britain and Germany sought to maintain a distinction between bombing military targets and civilian populations. The Nazis abandoned their restraints when they launched all-out attacks on British cities; their bombers killed about 40,000 noncombatants and wounded or made homeless many more between September 1940 and May 1941.[8]

The British responded in kind; in early 1942 they terminated their practice of "precision bombing," which, given the vagaries of weather conditions, the dangers of attacking well-defended objectives, and the inaccuracy of bombsights, had been an often futile attempt to hit specific military targets. Instead, they turned to nighttime "area bombing" of densely populated cities. In this way they hoped to undermine German morale and prevent noncombatants from working in factories that supplied the Nazi war machine, either by killing or wounding them, destroying their homes, or demolishing their workplaces.

After the United States entered the European war, its air forces, then a part of the Army, refused for a long time to adopt the British strategy. While recognizing the imprecision of precision bombing, they sought to minimize the impact on noncombatants by carrying out their sorties during the daytime and focusing on military targets. The distinctions were frequently lost in the heat of battle, and gradually the American air forces moved closer to the practice of area bombing, more graphically described as "terror bombing." On February 13–14, 1945, British and American planes deliberately practiced terror bombing in a massive assault on the German city of Dresden. Dresden had few targets of military significance; it was a center of culture that had largely escaped destruction during the war. As part of an effort to undermine German morale, the aerial attacks by Allied bombers gutted the city and killed about 35,000 people. Nevertheless, U.S. military officials insisted that they had not abandoned precision bombing and, insofar as possible, remained committed to sparing civilians from indiscriminate attacks from the air.

The evolution of American bombing strategies and practices led to the ambivalence that existed at the time that B-29s began their attacks on the Japanese islands. On the one hand, the official policy was still to attack military objectives and to avoid striking population centers. On the other hand, the very nature of strategic bombing meant that, sometimes accidentally and other times intentionally, homes, schools, hospitals, and other nonmilitary structures would be hit, with considerable loss of life among civilians. The problem of separating civilian and military targets was even more difficult in Japan than in Europe because of the significant amount of "home industry" in Japan. Nevertheless, the general in charge of the bomber command that flew B-29s over Japan, Haywood S. Hansell Jr., tried to maintain the distinction; he sought to destroy Japanese industry but not to raze residential areas.

The problem with Hansell's approach was that it did not work well, either in avoiding population centers or in disabling Japanese war industries. One advantage of the B-29s was that they could fly at altitudes that were beyond the range of Japanese antiaircraft guns and, at least initially, fighter planes. Therefore, they dropped bombs from as high as 30,000 feet above their targets. Unfortunately, at that altitude, their aim was wildly inaccurate. The bombs hit their targets only about 10 percent of the time and often landed instead in civilian sectors. Those difficulties were compounded by unfavorable weather and wind conditions that often prevailed in Japan. The results of the first B-29 raids were acutely disappointing, and in early 1945, the commanding general of the Army Air Forces, H. H. (Hap) Arnold, replaced Hansell with General Curtis E. LeMay.

When LeMay took command, Arnold pressed him to attack Japan with newly improved incendiary bombs that could be used to torch cities. Incendiaries promised to be particularly destructive in Japanese cities because of the density of their populations and the vulnerability of their wooden homes to fire. It was apparent that firebombing would not be restricted to military targets; the objective was to lay waste to major sections of the cities that were bombed. Hansell had resisted Arnold's pressure for firebombing, but LeMay, who remarked after the war that "there are no innocent civilians," looked for ways to use incendiaries most effectively.[9]

LeMay devised new tactics for using firebombs against Japan. He decided to launch an all-out nighttime attack on Tokyo in which a fleet of B-29s would drop bombs from low altitudes, enabling the planes to carry more bombs and to improve accuracy. LeMay also removed machine guns from the bombers to allow them to carry even more bombs. He recognized that this was a risky innovation, but he calculated that the Japanese would not be able to mount an effective defense if they were surprised by a low-altitude nighttime attack. The purpose of his plan, he said, was to hit Tokyo so hard that it would be "burned down—wiped right off the map."[10]

On the night of March 9, 1945, more than 300 B-29s took off from the Marianas on the 3,000-mile round trip to Tokyo. The first planes that reached the Japanese capital dropped incendiaries designed to start fires that would serve as markers in the target area for the bombers that followed. The target zone included industrial and commercial sites and densely populated residential districts with flimsy and highly flammable housing. Once the area was clearly delineated by flames, waves of B-29s dropped hundreds of tons of firebombs. They created a conflagration of monumental proportions, which was intensified by the winds that swept Tokyo that night. The fires consumed an area of about 16 square miles, created so much turbulence that they tossed low-flying planes around in the air, and killed so many Japanese that the stench of burning flesh sickened crews in the B-29s.

The firebombing of Tokyo took a fearful toll in human life. The residents of the target zone desperately sought shelter and safety, but little was to be found. Some fled to buildings that were sturdier than their homes, only to have bombs crash through the roofs and create inescapable infernos. Others waded into rivers or canals, but lost their lives when the water boiled. Many people burned to ashes, suffocated from the lack of oxygen, or died from carbon monoxide poisoning. "The very streets were rivers of fire," recalled one survivor. "Everywhere one could see flaming pieces of furniture exploding in the heat, while the people

FIGURE 2 Damage to Tokyo from firebombing by American bombers. (U.S. Army Air Corps, courtesy Harry S. Truman Library)

themselves blazed like matchsticks."[11] The number of people who died in the fire raid on March 9–10 is impossible to calculate with precision, but conservative estimates put the figure at more than 87,000. Another 41,000 were injured, and over 1 million lost their homes.[12]

LeMay followed the attack by firebombing other major cities as well as returning to Tokyo with more raids. Although the Army Air Forces maintained an official position that they had not adopted a policy of area bombing that targeted civilian populations, the firebombings of Japanese cities clearly demonstrated that attacks on noncombatants were neither unplanned nor operationally inadvertent. They were intended to shorten the war by destroying not only the factories that gave the Japanese the means to continue fighting but also to sabotage morale that gave them the will to continue fighting.

The bombing of the homeland was the latest scourge to strike Japan.

By the spring of 1945, its military strength was a pale shadow of the formidable machine that had raided Pearl Harbor and overrun vast expanses of East Asia. The once-proud navy had ceased to exist as an effective fighting force. The air corps could no longer claim technological superiority over American planes and had lost a large percentage of its skilled pilots. The training of new recruits was discontinued in March 1945 because of a lack of aviation fuel. The decline of the air force left Japanese cities poorly defended against American bombing attacks.

Despite heavy losses in its battles against American landings in the island campaign, the army was still large in numbers. But much of it remained bogged down on the Asian mainland or isolated on islands that American forces bypassed. A tight blockade—enforced by American carrier-based and land-based aircraft, submarines, and mines—cut Japan off from its sources of vital supplies, including staples such as foodstuffs and oil. It faced the grim prospect of diminishing stockpiles of goods that were essential not only to the war effort but to the very life of the nation. Civilian morale was shaken by the bombing of cities, the dwindling supplies, and the other heavy costs that the war assessed on the Japanese home front. Even the army was suffering from decreasing morale.

In April 1945, Admiral Baron Kantarō Suzuki became the premier of Japan, and one of his first acts was to instruct his chief cabinet secretary, Hisatsune Sakomizu, to prepare a report on Japan's ability to continue the war. Sakomizu's frank and somber survey held out no hope that the situation would improve or that Japan could carry on the fight long into the future. He concluded that transportation, shipping, communications, and industry had been so sharply curtailed that the national economy would grind to a virtual standstill. Food shortages were becoming serious, and Sakomizu predicted they would become acute by the end of 1945: "The people will have to get along on an absolute minimum of rice and salt required for subsistence, considering the severity of the air raids, difficulties in transportation, and the appearance of starvation conditions in the isolated sections of the nation." He warned Suzuki not only that was it "increasingly difficult to meet the requirements of total war," but also that the Japanese people were growing weary of the conflict and dissatisfied with their leaders. Although Sakomizu thought public morale was still high, he added that criticism of the government was increasingly evident and that morale would falter. "The people are losing confidence in their leaders," he observed, "and the gloomy omen of deterioration of public morale is present."[13]

The recognition that Japan was on the verge of defeat did not mean, however, that it was on the verge of surrender. Japanese military leaders had realized after the fall of Saipan in July 1944 that they could not win the war. "We can no longer direct the war," they concluded, "with any hope of success." Nevertheless, they fought on in hopes of undermining the American will to continue the war and securing better surrender terms. After deciding the war was a lost cause, they suggested that the "only course left is for Japan's one hundred million people to sacrifice their lives by charging the enemy to make them lose the will to fight."[14]

Gradually, as the American bombing and blockade took an increasingly heavy toll, some high officials of the Japanese government looked for ways to end the war promptly on satisfactory terms. By June 1945, their ranks were led by Foreign Minister Shigenori Tōgō and Lord Keeper of the Privy Seal Kōichi Kido, a boyhood friend and influential adviser of the Japanese emperor, Hirohito. Kido had concluded that "letting the Allied Forces into the home lands meant utter waste of human lives without the slightest hope of any kind." This argument was adamantly opposed by most military leaders. The key deliberations over Japan's position on continuing the war or seeking peace took place among the six members of the Supreme Council for the Direction of the War. Its members were, in addition to Tōgō and Premier Suzuki, War Minister Korechika Anami, Navy Minister Mitsumasa Yonai, Chief of the Army General Staff Yoshijiro Umezu, and Chief of the Navy General Staff Soemu Toyoda.

Despite the divisions within the Supreme Council over the issue of continuing the war or striving for peace, its members agreed that Japan's national polity must be preserved. Even those who favored ending the war would not surrender unless they received assurances that the emperor would be allowed to remain on his throne. The emperor was regarded in Japan as a deity whose removal from the throne or, even worse, trial as a war criminal was unthinkable. Constitutionally, the emperor, in the words of historian Daikichi Iro-kawa, "was a supreme authority with sovereign power over the entire Japanese imperial state," including "sole authority over [the] armed forces as their supreme commander."[15]

Hirohito was once depicted by most scholars as a passive and remote monarch who remained in the background while military zealots ran the country. Since his death in 1989, however, new evidence has come to light that has produced a different view. It is now clear that Hirohito actively participated in military planning and operational decisions during the war and that he long supported the objectives of his military leaders. In February 1945, for example, he rejected an appeal to move toward ending the war by remarking that this would be "very difficult unless we make one more military gain."[16]

As Japanese suffering from the war became increasingly widespread and increasingly apparent, Hirohito wavered in his position. On June 8, 1945, he agreed to the military's call for all-out resistance to an American invasion in which 100 million Japanese would join in a heroic last stand. Two weeks later, the emperor summoned the Supreme Council for the Direction of the War and made clear his desire to follow Kido's suggestion that Japan send "peace feelers" to Moscow as a way of trying to arrange an acceptable negotiated settlement. The emperor did not clearly decide between the competing views within the Supreme Council, and Japanese policies reflected his ambivalence and indecision.

While Japanese leaders deliberated, the bloodiest battle of the Pacific war took place on the island of Okinawa. Okinawa, 350 miles south of the main Japanese islands, was a key objective for American forces because it would serve as a staging area for an invasion of the Japanese homeland and as a site for air bases. On April 1, 1945—Easter Sunday—180,000 Marine and Army soldiers launched an assault on the island. They were supported and supplied by an armada of 1,200 ships, the largest fleet the United States had ever assembled, including 40 aircraft carriers, 18 battle-ships, and nearly 200 destroyers.[17] At first the invasion was surprisingly easy; the Japanese lacked the strength to try to meet the American troops on the beaches and throw them back. Instead they waited in extremely well-fortified and well-hidden bunkers, tunnels, and caves.

American troops quickly and efficiently took command of the lightly defended northern part of Okinawa. But within a week after the landings, those who advanced in the southern portions ran into fierce resistance. The Japanese fortifications were so well concealed that some Americans were sitting ducks when machine guns opened fire from a range of just a few feet. The battle was a desperate struggle to move ahead and stay alive in the face of murderous cross fire from a determined foe. "Every day you lived for one day more," recalled one veteran. "That was where your horizon ended, the limit of your plans." One of his comrades was even more graphic in his description of the fighting on Okinawa: "Time had no meaning. Life had no meaning. . . . I had resigned from the human race. I just wanted to kill."[18] Gradually and painfully, the Americans overcame Japanese defenses and gained control of the island.

But the costs were high—about 7,000 members of the Army and Marines were killed or missing in action.

While the Marines and the Army were slowly fighting a tortuous campaign, the Navy was also enduring losses of unprecedented magnitude. The Japanese had managed to muster about 700 airplanes, many of which were used as explosive missiles aimed at American ships by suicide pilots. The deterioration of the Japanese air force was so advanced by 1945 that it adopted a new tactic of using planes as bombs rather than as bombers. The pilots of the suicide missions, the famous kamikazes, received minimal training before departing on their one-way flights. The heavy dependence on kamikazes was a sign of Japanese weakness and desperation as well as the die-hard attitude that was prominent within the military leadership and among the pilots who flew the planes. In many cases the kamikazes were ineffective; they often failed to find their targets or missed their targets once they located them. But all too frequently they successfully carried out their missions. They sank 13 destroyers and damaged dozens of other American ships in the battle for Okinawa. The kamikazes struck so many destroyers that the men on one hung a huge arrow on the deck with a sign that read "Carriers this way."[19] The carriers also suffered, as did all the ships in the fleet, from the attacks and from the fear, tension, and fatigue that they caused.

By the time the battle of Okinawa ended on June 21, about 5,000 American sailors had been killed and another 5,000 wounded, a total higher than that of any other naval engagement in American history. The combined American casualties of 12,000 killed and missing and another 60,000 wounded far exceeded those of any other battle in the Pacific war. Japanese military forces suffered at least 70,000 deaths; in addition, as many as 150,000 Okinawan noncombatants lost their lives, including those who killed their families and themselves to avoid capture by Americans. One sign of weakening morale in the Japanese army was that 7,400 soldiers surrendered. This number was still a small percentage of the Japanese units on the island, and many who surrendered were Okinawans who had been dragooned into the army. Nevertheless, it was a much larger percentage than those who had surrendered at Iwo Jima, and it suggested that an increasing number of Japanese soldiers had decided to take their chances with the reputedly barbaric enemy rather than die for the emperor.[20]

By the end of June 1945, it had been apparent for some time to both American and Japanese leaders that the outcome of the war would be

FIGURE 3 Japanese kamikaze plane attacking the USS *Missouri* off Okinawa, April 1945. (National Archives 80-G-315811-A)

certain defeat for Japan. It was also becoming distressingly obvious to the Japanese people, because the propaganda of the government could not conceal the ease with which American planes bombed Japanese cities. While Japan became increasingly defenseless against the onslaught, American forces gained in strength. But they still confronted the grim prospect of another bloody invasion. The fundamental problem for the governments of both the United States and Japan was to find an acceptable way to end the war. The Japanese government was paralyzed by indecision and dissension. The United States was committed to a total victory at the lowest possible cost in American lives. Even if the defeat of Japan was inevitable, the costs and the means of forcing the surrender remained uncertain.

4

Paths to Victory

As the Okinawa campaign was drawing to a close in June 1945, President Truman asked the Joint Chiefs of Staff to provide him with information and their judgment on several key issues regarding the achievement of final victory in the war with Japan. To plan for future military actions and to prepare for the upcoming summit conference with Soviet Premier Stalin and British Prime Minister Churchill, he requested their estimates of the time required to force a Japanese surrender and the costs in American casualties for both an invasion of Japan and the continuation of the bombings and blockade without an invasion. The president also wanted the Joint Chiefs to tell him "exactly what we want the Russians to do" to speed the end of the war. Truman made his primary concerns clear to the White House chief of staff, Admiral William D. Leahy. "It is his intention to make his decisions on the campaign with the purpose of economizing to the maximum extent possible in the loss of American lives," Leahy told the Joint Chiefs. "Economy in the use of time and in money cost is comparatively unimportant."[1] On June 17, Truman confided to his diary that deciding between authorizing an invasion and relying solely on the bombing and blockade as the better means to bring the war to a conclusion was his "hardest decision to date."[2]

The Joint Chiefs presented their views to the president at a meeting at the White House on June 18. Those in attendance were Secretary of War Stimson, Assistant Secretary of War John J. McCloy, Secretary of the Navy James V. Forrestal, and the members of the Joint Chiefs—Leahy, General Marshall, Admiral Ernest J. King, and General Ira C. Eaker, representing General Arnold for the Army Air Forces. Marshall, speaking for the Joint Chiefs, recommended that preparations be made to launch an invasion of Kyushu, the southernmost of the Japanese islands, with a target date of November 1, 1945. A second phase of the invasion of Japan would take place at a later time against Honshu, the main island, on which Tokyo is located. Marshall read from a paper drawn up by the Joint Chiefs: "The Kyushu operation is essential to a strategy of strangulation and appears to be the least costly worthwhile operation following Okinawa." He added his personal opinion that "air power alone was not sufficient to put the Japanese out of the war."[3]

The other officials at the meeting expressed agreement with Marshall's conclusion that plans for the invasion of Kyushu should proceed. The Joint Chiefs did not provide clear guidance on two of the other matters on which Truman had sought information. They did not address his request for an assessment of how long it might take to produce a Japanese surrender. They hedged on the crucial issue of casualty figures. The Joint Chiefs obliquely projected about 31,000 casualties, based on their belief that "the first 30 days in Kyushu should not exceed the price we have paid for Luzon." They refused, however, to present any more precise figures. Leahy offered his view that an estimate could be derived from multiplying the percentage of troops involved in the Okinawa campaign who became casualties by the number expected to participate in the assault on Kyushu. But he did not undertake any computations at the meeting and Truman did not press him to do so.[4] On the question of Soviet participation in the war, Marshall maintained that it was highly desirable. Everyone at the meeting concurred that Soviet entry into the war against Japan "would have considerable influence," but no one suggested that this alone would make an invasion unnecessary.[5]

The question of Soviet participation received less attention than the exploration of other alternatives to an invasion. Stimson, who was ill and had dragged himself out of bed to attend the meeting, said he agreed with the Joint Chiefs that preparations for an invasion of Kyushu should proceed. But he hoped that the attack would not be required to bring about the Japanese surrender. He remarked that "there was a large submerged class in Japan" that did not favor the war but would "fight tenaciously" for their homeland. Stimson thought the war might end by some other means, though at this time he did not specify what the alternatives were. Leahy was less reticent; he declared that the United States should not hold out for an unconditional surrender. This, he feared, "would result only in making the Japanese desperate and thereby increase our casualty lists."[6]

Truman responded that he did not believe that he could take any action at the time "to change public opinion" on the question of unconditional surrender. On American casualties, the issue that concerned him most, he said that he hoped "there was a possibility of preventing an Okinawa from one end of Japan to the other." He announced that he "considered the Kyushu plan all right from a military standpoint" and that the "Joint Chiefs should go ahead with it." He withheld a final decision on authorizing the attack on Honshu until a later time. The president observed that the conference had "cleared up a great many points in his mind and that he now felt satisfied and reassured." According to the minutes of the meeting, those in attendance "discussed certain other matters," presumably the still highly secret atomic bomb project.[7]

The June 18 meeting was a critical step in planning for future actions to force a Japanese surrender and in highlighting the opinions, assumptions, and concerns of key American policymakers. Although the minutes of the meeting are at times frustratingly ambiguous, they make clear the thinking of Truman and his military advisers on a number of important points. The president and his top lieutenants recognized that Japan was nearing collapse, but they remained uncertain of the best way to achieve an early surrender. They were convinced that they must press ahead with planning for the invasion of Japan as the best option for ending the war. They expressed little doubt at the meeting that the attack on Kyushu would prove to be essential. They were hopeful, however, that the second phase of the invasion, the assault on Honshu, would be unnecessary. Marshall commented that "Kyushu was a necessity" and after it had "been arranged for, the decision as to further action could be made later."[8] Finally, Truman and his advisers sought to reduce American casualties to the minimum required to win a decisive victory over Japan.

While the discussion at the June 18 meeting demonstrated a consensus among Truman's top advisers on several important questions, it obscured or understated differing opinions on other issues. One vital issue on which the president was not fully informed was casualty estimates. The Joint Chiefs had declined to present any specific estimates at the meeting on the grounds that "our experience in the Pacific war is so diverse as to casualties that it is considered wrong to give any estimates in numbers." Therefore, they had only gone so far as to cite American losses in previous battles of the Pacific war and to suggest that casualties in the first 30 days of an invasion of Kyushu would not exceed those suffered in capturing Luzon (31,000 killed, wounded, and missing).[9]

The Joint Chiefs, however, had recently received an estimate of much higher casualties in an invasion. In preparing for the meeting, the Joint War Plans Committee, which included officials from both the Army and the Navy, had drafted a report for the Joint Chiefs that projected a total of about 132,500 casualties (killed, wounded, and missing) for the Kyushu operation. They calculated that about 25,000 of those casualties would be fatalities (the ratio of deaths to casualties during the war was approximately 1:4 to 1:5). The plans committee further predicted that if the invasion of Honshu became necessary, American forces would suffer another 87,500 casualties, including 21,000 deaths. Thus, in the committee's opinion, the two phases of the invasion of Japan would cost about 46,000 American deaths and another 174,000 wounded and missing. The plans committee recommended that the invasion of Honshu, if required, begin around March 1, 1946; it suggested that in the worst case, the war would be over by the end of 1946.[10]

Marshall was convinced that the invasion of Kyushu, rather than sole reliance on bombing and the blockade, was the best way to achieve an early Japanese surrender. He seems to have been concerned that the casualty estimates of the Joint War Plans Committee would alarm the president and undermine his support for an invasion. In preparing for the June 18 meeting, Marshall also requested an estimate from General Douglas MacArthur, commander of the U.S. Army in the Pacific. MacArthur cabled a projection that was remarkably close to that of the plans committee—105,000 battle and another 12,600 nonbattle casualties in the Kyushu operation. Marshall immediately asked for a clarification of the basis for that figure. MacArthur, who was anxious to lead the invasion of Kyushu, wired back that the estimate was "purely academic" and that he anticipated a smaller number of casualties. He added: "I regard the [Kyushu] operation as the most economical one in effort and lives that is possible."[11] Marshall read MacArthur's second cable but did not mention the larger casualty estimates in the meeting with the president. The figure of 31,000 casualties in the first 30 days was apparently the only one Truman heard before the end of the war. There is no evidence that he received information from high-ranking military officials that an invasion of Japan would cost as many as 500,000 to 1 million American casualties or deaths, as he and some of his advisers claimed after the war.[12]

The consensus that prevailed at the June 18 meeting not only side-stepped the question of casualties but also downplayed differing views among high-level advisers about the best way to force a Japanese surrender. Before and after the meeting with the president, they debated alternatives to the invasion of Japan. The question they weighed was the likelihood that one or more of the alternatives would end the war on satisfactory terms sooner and at a lower cost in U.S. casualties. There were three options other than an invasion that were seriously considered by American policymakers, all of which were mentioned at the June 18 meeting but not discussed at length.

The first of the alternatives was to continue and intensify the bombing and blockade of Japan in hopes that this would force a Japanese surrender without an invasion. Truman called the June 18 meeting for the purpose of choosing between exclusive reliance on this approach or authorizing an invasion, and after his advisers presented a united front for the invasion, he approved it. But the recommendation of the Joint Chiefs at the meeting did not make clear the conviction of some authorities in the Army Air Forces and the Navy that unrelenting aerial attacks combined with the naval blockade were the best way to bring about the Japanese surrender. They insisted that an invasion of Japan was unnecessary and the price in casualties would be unacceptably high. General LeMay was a leading advocate of this position. He contended in April 1945 that air power could force the Japanese to surrender within six months, which would have ended the war before the invasion of Kyushu began. Although a number of his colleagues felt the same way, his superior, General Arnold, was less certain. In the June 18 meeting, General Eaker, representing the Army Air Forces, told the president that Arnold "expressed complete agreement" with Marshall on the need for the invasion of Kyushu.[13]

LeMay and other air force leaders saw the bombing of Japan not only as a way to end the war but also to underscore the importance of air power. They hoped to become a separate department of the armed forces after the war; LeMay asserted that their campaign against Japan gave them "the opportunity of proving the power of the strategic air arm."[14] Therefore, LeMay's predictions in the spring of 1945 and the claims of many of his colleagues after the war that bombing with conventional weapons would have forced the Japanese surrender were colored by bureaucratic considerations.

Although LeMay offered a way to end the war that might cost fewer American casualties than an invasion, Marshall was skeptical of the position he advanced. Marshall did not believe that air power had been decisive in defeating Germany, and he thought it would be less effective against Japan. He feared that the bombing and blockade approach, even if it ultimately proved to be successful, would take much longer than an invasion to achieve final victory. The Joint Intelligence Committee, which included representatives from the Army and Navy and reported to the Joint Chiefs of Staff, concluded in April 1945 that the amount of time required to force an unconditional surrender by depending on bombing and a blockade without an invasion ranged "from a few months to a great many years." Its best estimate was that such an approach would take at least until the middle of 1946 to end the war. In that amount of time American casualties could exceed the cost of an invasion.[15]

There is no way of knowing, of course, whether Marshall's or LeMay's arguments would have proven more accurate, but neither the Joint Chiefs nor Truman's other military advisers took issue with Marshall's analysis. In their view, bombing and the blockade were more a supplement than an alternative to an invasion. They did not believe that air power alone would bring about the surrender on American terms at the lowest cost or the earliest possible time. To Marshall the question of timing was vital. "War is the most terrible tragedy of the human race," he told the American Legion in September 1944, "and it should not be prolonged an hour longer than is absolutely necessary."[16]

In addition, Marshall's position reflected the uncertainty that prevailed among military leaders about how long they could count on public support for the war effort in the United States. Both sides of the argument over the better approach to defeating Japan expressed concern that a significant portion of the population would clamor for a speedy end before a complete victory was achieved. Admiral King, for example, had worried out loud in 1944 "that the American people will weary of [the war with Japan] quickly, and that pressure will force a negotiated peace before the Japs are really licked." Once the war with Germany was won, the push to bring American soldiers home and to relieve domestic shortages increased. Fred M. Vinson, director of the Office of War Mobilization and Reconversion, informed the Joint Chiefs in May 1945 that scarcities of food and clothing, combined with labor strife, caused him to worry about conversion to a peacetime economy. He said that he was "afraid of unrest in the country" and thought "that the next three to six months will make a vital difference in our future economy." Vinson appealed to the Joint Chiefs to reduce their demands on production, if possible. Marshall responded that until the war ended, "production must be kept up."[17] But the problems that Vinson cited placed an additional premium on the need to bring about a Japanese surrender as soon as possible.

A second possible alternative to an invasion stirred little debate among U.S. military planners or policymakers (though it later created a great deal of controversy among scholars). This alternative was to wait for the Soviet Union to enter the war against Japan, which Stalin had promised at Yalta and reaffirmed in his talks with Harry Hopkins, in anticipation that this would produce a surrender. Securing Stalin's pledge of Soviet participation in the war had been one of Roosevelt's primary objectives at Yalta. American military strategists viewed Soviet belligerency as a means to tie down Japanese troops in Manchuria so that they could not be shipped home to defend against an American invasion. By the spring of 1945, however, the dominance of the U.S. Navy in Japanese waters appeared likely to prevent the movement of troops between the Asian mainland and Japan. This made Soviet entry into the war much less vital for the success of an American invasion. Nevertheless, American planners still regarded a Soviet attack on Japanese forces in Manchuria as useful for its shock value. They hoped that Soviet entry would help demonstrate to both the Japanese people and the government that their cause was hopeless.

American military officials did not suggest, however, that Soviet participation in the war with Japan was sufficient in itself to bring about a surrender. Marshall's staff addressed this question in a memorandum to Secretary of War Stimson on June 4, 1945. "The point in our military progress at which the Japanese will accept defeat and agree to our terms is unpredictable," it read. "Probably it will take Russian entry into the war, coupled with a landing, or imminent threat of landing, on Japan proper by us, to convince them of the hopelessness of their position."[18] American planners viewed the prospect of Soviet entry as helpful in shortening the war but not as essential for winning it or as a substitute for the invasion. At the June 18 meeting, Truman commented that one of his objectives at the upcoming summit conference "would be to get from Russia all the assistance in the war that was possible," and he wanted to be able "to occupy the strongest possible position in the discussions." Admiral King cautioned that "regardless of the desirability of the Russians entering the war, they were not indispensable and he did not think we should go so far as to beg them to come in."[19]

Soviet entry into the war would be advantageous for the war effort, but the benefits would come at a cost from a diplomatic perspective. It would expand Soviet presence, power, and influence in China and other parts of Asia, which was not a welcome prospect at a time when tensions between the United States and the Soviet Union were increasing over contentious issues in Europe. Acting Secretary of State Joseph C. Grew articulated this concern in May 1945: "Already Russia is showing us—in Poland, Rumania, Bulgaria, Hungary, Austria, Czechoslovakia, and Yugoslavia—the future world pattern that she envisions and will aim to create. . . . Once Russia is in the war against Japan, then Mongolia, Manchuria, and Korea will eventually slip into Russia's orbit, to be followed in due course by China and eventually Japan."[20]

Another possible alternative to an invasion received the most attention and support within the Truman administration. It was to mitigate the American demand for unconditional surrender by allowing the Japanese to retain the institution of the emperor. The policy of unconditional surrender was a part of Truman's legacy from Roosevelt. Drawing on the lessons of World War I, Roosevelt had sought to make certain that America's enemies could not claim they had not lost the war on the battlefield. Mindful that the Nazis had exploited the false charge that the Kaiser's army had been defeated by a stab in the back from its own citizens, he wrote in 1942: "We have no intention of concluding this war with any kind of armistice or treaty. Germany must surrender unconditionally."[21] After consideration of the policy by the State Department and the Joint Chiefs and consultation with the British, Roosevelt announced the policy during a meeting with Churchill in Casablanca in 1943. The demand for unconditional surrender was not intended as a threat to enslave the citizens of America's enemies. Rather, its purpose was to promote the elimination of the war power of Germany, Italy, and Japan and "the destruction of a philosophy . . . which is based on the conquest and subjugation of other peoples."[22]

In the spring of 1945 a growing number of American policymakers favored a modification or clarification of the unconditional surrender policy because they feared that it would prolong the war. They wanted to make clear to the Japanese that surrender would not necessarily mean the abolition of the imperial institution or the punishment of Hirohito. They were persuaded that the Japanese would fight to a bitter and desperate finish, with a higher cost in American lives, if the emperor faced trial as a war criminal and/or loss of his throne. A report prepared by MacArthur's staff in 1944 warned that "to dethrone, or hang, the Emperor would cause a tremendous and violent reaction from all Japanese." It added: "Hanging of the Emperor to them would be comparable to the crucifixion of Christ to us. All would fight to die like ants."[23]

The most fervent advocate of softening the policy of unconditional surrender to allow the emperor to remain as a constitutional monarch with sharply diminished powers was Acting Secretary of State Grew, who had served as the American ambassador in Tokyo for the 10 years before World War II. He was an expert on and admirer of Japan, which was an important part of the reason that he sought to find a way to end the war short of an invasion. He was also deeply suspicious of Soviet intentions and thought that permitting Japan to keep an emperor, though not necessarily the reigning emperor, would help it to regain order and stability in the postwar era. This would make Japan less vulnerable to

Soviet inroads. Grew argued that insisting on unconditional surrender would be a disaster for both the United States and Japan. He told Truman on May 28 that the "Japanese are a fanatical people and are capable of fighting to the last ditch and the last man." If they were assured, however, that the institution of the emperor would not be destroyed, he believed they would be much more inclined to surrender. Otherwise, he counseled, "surrender will be highly unlikely." Truman indicated that he agreed by responding that "his own thoughts had been following the same line."[24] A short time later, however, he issued a Memorial Day message that called for Japan's unconditional surrender.

Although Truman did not follow Grew's advice, the arguments of the acting secretary of state won other important converts. Stimson, McCloy, Leahy, Forrestal, Marshall, and Undersecretary of the Navy Bard agreed with Grew that modifying the unconditional surrender policy to allow the Japanese the opportunity to keep the imperial institution might help shorten the war and perhaps avoid the need for an invasion. They did not embrace this position with equal enthusiasm or confidence, and they held differing views about the proper timing for issuing a statement. Nevertheless, they accepted Grew's reasoning that offering to soften the requirement for unconditional surrender could provide military and diplomatic benefits.

Stimson told the president on July 2 that Japan was "susceptible to reason" and was "not a nation composed wholly of mad fanatics of an entirely different mentality than ours." He urged the publication of a statement making clear that although the United States insisted Japan rid itself of "militaristic influences," it did not wish "to extirpate the Japanese as a race or destroy them as a nation." Stimson advised that if the statement also assured the Japanese that "we do not exclude a constitutional monarchy under her present dynasty, it would substantially add to the chances of acceptance." Stimson recorded in his diary that Truman was "apparently acquiescent" with his comments.[25]

The president's attitude toward modifying unconditional surrender was unclear, probably reflecting his own ambivalence. When he indicated to Grew and Stimson that he supported their views on unconditional surrender, he was at least partly indulging his habit of expressing vague agreement with whomever he was talking to at a given moment. But he seems to have been genuinely uncertain of where he stood on the issue. Although the position of Grew, Stimson, and their colleagues was in some ways appealing, the impact of implementing it was unpredictable and potentially harmful.

On the international front, offering to back off the demand for unconditional surrender could prove to be counterproductive, by strengthening the hand of the die-hard military faction in the Japanese government. If the United States appeared to weaken its demands in the wake of the difficulties its troops endured and the casualties they suffered during the Okinawa campaign, it would enhance the credibility of the argument that the Americans must be confronted with all-out resistance to the invasion of Japan. The members of the Supreme Council for the Direction of the War who opposed peace initiatives contended that inflicting a heavy toll on American forces could win more favorable terms. War Minister Anami, according to the later testimony of Lord Keeper of the Privy Seal Kido, posed the question in a way that left no doubt about his answer: "Wouldn't it be to our advantage if peace were established after we had given the enemy a terrible beating in the decisive battle on the homeland?"[26] Thus, an offer by the United States to modify its policy could backfire by making it even more difficult to secure a surrender. State Department officials worried that the "steadily mounting public clamor for a statement of our proposed terms" would "create in Japan the impression that we are weakening in our determination" and "retard any movement in Japan to force the leaders to accept unconditional surrender." Stimson, despite his support for offering Japan the opportunity to keep the emperor, opposed an immediate statement to that effect for fear of strengthening the position of the militants.[27]

Military leaders seemed even more concerned about how moderating unconditional surrender might affect public support for the war in the United States. They took a cautious position on changing the policy; they saw potential advantages but also recognized possible drawbacks. Marshall's staff, for example, suggested that clarifying unconditional surrender had "definite merit" if it were done "in the nature of an ultimatum" and not in a way to "invite negotiation." Otherwise, they warned, "there is the danger of seriously impairing the will to war of the people of the United States, with consequent damaging effect on our war effort, prolongation of the war and unnecessarily increased cost in human lives; or alternately acceptance of a compromise peace." The Joint Chiefs worried that a Japanese proposal for a negotiated peace at a time when large numbers of American troops were waiting for redeployment from Europe to the Pacific could severely undermine American morale. Marshall told Stimson that he endorsed a proposal to revise the demand for unconditional surrender to "complete defeat and permanent destruction of the war making power of Japan." But he cautioned that "we should ... diligently avoid any impression that we are growing soft" because it might increase the difficulties of "holding ... our own people" and ending the war "at the earliest possible date."[28]

The concerns of military leaders that backing away from unconditional surrender was risky were perhaps based on their knowledge that, from all indications, the policy was enormously popular with the American people as a means of averting another war in the future. In order to maintain support for making the sacrifices required for a decisive victory over Japan, the Office of War Information (OWI), a wartime agency whose functions included keeping public morale high, promoted the importance of unconditional surrender. It suggested that the demand for unconditional surrender was the only way to prevent a revival of Japanese imperialism. "Only [Japan's] unconditional surrender can lead to the smashing of [its] militaristic hopes and ambitions," an OWI circular declared in June 1945. It warned that Japan hoped to take advantage of war weariness in the United States to achieve a compromise settlement. Japan "will seek a compromise peace that will leave intact her present ruling clique and enough territory and industrial strength to begin again a career of aggressive expansion," the circular predicted. The fear of allowing Japan to renew its aggression, which OWI cited and heightened with its own appeals, reinforced the strong public support for unconditional surrender in the spring of 1945.[29]

Indications of the popularity of unconditional surrender were unmistakably clear. When Truman addressed Congress for the first time after becoming president and reaffirmed his support for the unconditional surrender policy, he received a rousing ovation. A Gallup poll taken in June 1945 asked whether the United States should accept a surrender with the stipulation that it would not occupy Japan or whether it should continue the war until the enemy was "completely beaten." By a margin of nine to one, respondents favored doing what was necessary for a complete victory. The emperor was reviled by most Americans, as another poll demonstrated when it asked about whether the emperor should be punished. It found that 33 percent of those who responded thought the emperor should be executed and another 17 percent wanted to put him on trial; only 4 percent favored no punishment.[30]

The overwhelming support for unconditional surrender and retribution against the emperor meant that Truman was taking a chance if he decided to change the policy. He was torn between differing views. On the one hand, virtually all of his key advisers backed the modification of unconditional surrender when the timing was appropriate if it did not allow the Japanese the opportunity to hold out for a negotiated settlement. On the other hand, such action carried substantial risks—it could strengthen the position of the Japanese militarists, undermine morale at home, and create significant political hazards for the president. The one adviser who opposed modifying unconditional surrender, Byrnes, was acutely conscious of political currents, and his position reinforced Truman's own political instincts. Changing a popular policy and potentially prolonging the war was a chancy and potentially disastrous venture. As a result, Truman vacillated.[31]

The proponents of moderating the policy of unconditional surrender received encouraging information on July 13, when American intercepts decoded a Japanese diplomatic message from Foreign Minister Tōgō to the Japanese ambassador to the Soviet Union, Naotake Satō. The message read in part: "His Majesty the Emperor, mindful of the fact that the present war daily brings greater evil and sacrifice upon the peoples of all belligerent powers, desires from his heart that it may be quickly terminated."[32] Tōgō went on to say that the major impediment to peace was the American (and British) insistence on unconditional surrender.

The Japanese government had decided to ask the Soviet Union for its friendly intervention in questions relating to the end of the war. The Soviets were still officially neutral in the Pacific war and were therefore the only nation on which Japan's Supreme Council for the Direction of the War could agree as a possible source of assistance. The military members of the council who wanted a last-ditch "decisive battle" adamantly opposed any direct contact between Japan and the United States; if their wishes were not met, they could resign from the cabinet and delay any further peace initiatives. The sharp divisions within the Japanese government were highlighted by the reasons that the competing factions wanted to approach the Soviet Union. The die-hard military representatives hoped that the Soviets could be convinced to continue a neutral stance or—a sign of how far out of touch with reality they were—to provide aid in Japan's final defense of the homeland. The peace faction within the Supreme Council hoped that the Soviets could be persuaded to act as mediators in bringing about a negotiated settlement to the war.

To fulfill their objectives, they had no place they could turn to except Moscow. American codebreakers had decoded Japanese diplomatic messages in 1939 and, since that time, had read traffic going to and from the Japanese foreign ministry. The decrypted messages were known as MAGIC. Through the wonders of MAGIC, American policymakers could follow the communications between Tōgō in Tokyo and Satō in Moscow.

The July 13 message that the emperor wanted to end the war quickly and that the main obstacle to a settlement was unconditional surrender seemed to support the position of American officials who favored allowing the Japanese the opportunity to keep the imperial institution. But the meaning of the message was unclear to those who intercepted it. The Army's highest-ranking intelligence officer, General John Weckerling, told Marshall and his staff he was very doubtful that the message was a genuine peace initiative. Weckerling had served in the American embassy in Tokyo from 1928 to 1932 and again from 1934 to 1938, and his experience in and knowledge of Japan gave additional weight to his opinions. He outlined three possible interpretations of Tōgō's cable. The first was that the "Emperor has personally intervened and brought his will to bear in favor of peace in spite of military opposition." The chances of this seemed "remote." The second interpretation was that "conservative groups close to the Throne, including some high ranking Army and Navy men, have triumphed over militaristic elements." This seemed to be "a possibility." The third interpretation was that the "Japanese governing clique is making a well-coordinated, united effort to stave off defeat believing (a) that Russian intervention can be bought by the proper price, and (b) that an attractive Japanese peace offer will appeal to war weariness in the United States." This pessimistic view seemed to be "quite probably the motivating force behind the Japanese moves." Weckerling's analysis was not limited to military circles. He noted that Grew, the most outspoken advocate of modifying unconditional surrender, agreed with his conclusions.[33]

If MAGIC could not make the meaning of Tōgō's message about the emperor's desire for peace clear, it could show beyond a reasonable doubt the lack of consensus within the Japanese government on the question of ending the war. This was a strong indication that offering to allow the imperial institution to remain was not sufficient in itself to induce a Japanese surrender. The Supreme Council for the Direction of the War was unable even to agree on proposals to present to the Soviets. Ambassador Satō voiced his frustration in his responses to Tōgō about the failure of his government to define its objectives or its terms in seeking Soviet intervention. He complained about "phrases beautiful but somewhat remote from the facts and empty in content." He advised that the Japanese government must first "firmly resolve to terminate the war" and realize that even if the Soviets agreed to mediate, the negotiated peace would "very closely approximate unconditional surrender." Satō seemed incredulous about the military's hopes that the Soviets might assist in their battle against an invasion. "I believe it is no exaggeration to say," he cabled Tokyo, "that the possibility of getting the Soviet Union to join our side and go along with our reasoning is next to nothing."[34] When American leaders read the diplomatic exchanges between Tokyo and Moscow, they could hardly help but conclude that the Japanese government was too divided and too indecisive about its own position to quit the war on the basis of a modest revision of the unconditional surrender policy.

In addition to the approach to the Soviets, ill-defined as it was, there were several informal Japanese peace feelers. Starting in April 1945 and continuing into the summer, midlevel Japanese officials in Switzerland, acting through intermediaries, suggested to Allen Dulles, director of the Office of Strategic Services in Bern, that their government was interested in a negotiated peace. They reported that the major stumbling block was the demand for unconditional surrender and indicated that a guarantee of the imperial institution might bring about an early peace. It soon became apparent that the Japanese diplomats were not acting with the authority of their government and that their offers held no official standing. Indeed, their appeals to Tokyo for instructions on arranging negotiations were long ignored and then dismissed. The lack of response from the Japanese government was further evidence that it was not ready for serious peace overtures.

What American leaders suspected about Japanese motives and knew about the bitter dissension within the Japanese government made the idea of modifying unconditional surrender seem at best an uncertain route to peace. If the Japanese had been prepared to surrender on the basis that the imperial institution be retained, they could have sent a clear signal to that effect to the United States, which almost certainly would have found the single condition acceptable. But the Japanese government was so torn by discord that it could not agree to make such an appeal, and instead it drifted toward disaster. The indecision of the Japanese Supreme Council for the Direction of the War reflected the ambivalence of the emperor, even after the fall of Okinawa. A short time before Tōgō's message of July 13 stating that Hirohito wanted the war to be "quickly terminated," the emperor had signaled that he wanted to continue the fighting to take advantage of an "opportunity for victory." He supported the idea of a new offensive in China.[35] His mixed feelings and contradictory statements about ending the war mirrored Truman's vacillation over whether to soften the policy of unconditional surrender. In that context, the chances of achieving peace with a negotiated settlement appear to have been remote.

Truman's decision to authorize the invasion of Kyushu, despite his recognition of its potentially high costs, was prompted by his belief that the available alternatives were burdened with military, diplomatic, and political risks that were unacceptable. None of the three options—continuing and intensifying the bombing and blockade, waiting for Soviet entry into the war, or modifying unconditional surrender—seemed certain, or even likely, to end the war decisively sooner and at a lower cost than an invasion. Using a combination of those approaches would not have eliminated their individual drawbacks. The primary American war objective was to win a complete victory *and* to keep U.S. casualties to a minimum, and the three alternative approaches seemed less promising for accomplishing those ends than did an invasion.

There was, however, a fourth alternative that might ease the president's dilemma—the atomic bomb. If the bomb worked, it provided a possible means to speed the end of the war without an invasion and without taking the risks that reduced the appeal of the other options. Truman and his advisers proceeded in their planning as if the bomb did not exist, but those who knew about it hoped that a successful test would lead to the accomplishment of their goals at a much lower cost than the existing alternatives.

In the summer of 1945, the Truman administration was not looking for ways to avoid using the bomb. It was seeking ways to end the war without an invasion of Japan. The various paths to victory that it considered were treated in that context, and not, as they are often discussed by scholars, as alternatives to the bomb. There was very little deliberation over what to do with the bomb once it was ready for deployment; existing evidence shows only two instances in which high-level officials weighed the question of how the bomb should be used.

The first occurred in a brief conversation between Stimson, McCloy, and Marshall on May 29, 1945. The subject of their discussion was "methods of concluding the war with minimum casualties," which led to consideration of gas warfare as well as the use of atomic weapons. Marshall suggested that atomic bombs should be dropped not on civilian targets but on "straight military objectives such as a large naval installation." If that did not have the desired effect, he proposed that the United States "designate a number of large manufacturing areas from which the people would be warned to leave." By issuing a warning, Marshall submitted, the United States could "offset . . . the opprobrium which might follow from an ill considered employment" of atomic weapons. Marshall's reflections apparently made little impression on Stimson and McCloy; they did not follow up on his ideas about the use of the bomb and he never raised them again.[36]

The issue of the use of the bomb was also discussed briefly and informally by members of the Interim Committee. The conversation took place for about 10 minutes during the lunch break of the committee's meeting on May 31, 1945. Somebody—probably Byrnes—asked whether a "harmless demonstration" of the bomb might be an effective way to demonstrate its power before it was used against a Japanese city. A number of leading Manhattan Project scientists considered the question but concluded, as Oppenheimer put it, that a demonstration would not be "sufficiently spectacular" to make the Japanese surrender.[37] Further, the demonstration shot could backfire if the bomb failed to go off, if the plane were shot down, or if the Japanese moved American prisoners into the test site. After deciding that a demonstration of the bomb was not advisable, the Interim Committee arrived at its recommendation that the best target for the atomic bomb "would be a vital war plant employing a large number of workers and closely surrounded by workers' homes."[38] In late June and early July of 1945, as American policymakers sought ways to end the war at the lowest cost in American casualties and Truman prepared to confer with Churchill and Stalin, the atomic bomb was a looming but still indefinite presence. Groves's assurances to Truman in April that a bomb fueled with uranium 235 would be ready for use around August 1 were not enough in themselves to serve as a basis for American planning. Truman and his advisers waited for a test that they hoped would prove the atomic bomb would be available as a weapon that might shorten the war with Japan and strengthen the president's negotiating position when he met with Churchill and Stalin.

5

Truman and the Bomb at Potsdam

When President Truman left the United States aboard a naval cruiser on July 7, 1945, to travel to Potsdam, a suburb of devastated Berlin, he was not looking forward to meeting with Generalissimo Stalin and Prime Minister Churchill. "Talked to Bess last night and the night before," he confided to his diary the night he departed. "She wasn't happy about my going to see Mr. Russia and Mr. Great Britain—neither am I." The president went on to write: "How I hate this trip! But I have to make it—win, lose or draw—and we must win." He expressed the same sentiments in a letter to Mrs. Truman the same day: "I sure dread this trip, worse than anything I've had to face."[1]

Truman's anxiety about attending the conference was understandable. He was still a novice at his job and still learning the complexities of the many problems he faced. He was traveling to meet and doubtlessly disagree on important issues with two crusty and renowned leaders who must have seemed larger than life, even to the president of the United States. He was determined to protect American interests but worried about how successful he would be in jousting with his formidable, tenacious, and experienced counterparts. Truman sought to educate himself about the background of the questions that would be discussed at Potsdam and about the proceedings of previous wartime summit conferences. He told Mrs. Truman that he would "have to depend on Leahy and Byrnes" and that despite hating to take the trip, he recognized that he was "elected to do a job." He added rather wistfully: "Here's hoping I can do it."[2]

The agenda for Potsdam featured many complex and divisive issues. Ending the Pacific war was only one of many questions facing Truman, Churchill, and Stalin. The focus of the conference was the future of Europe: the key matters to be discussed included admission of Italy into the United Nations; diplomatic recognition of Bulgaria, Rumania, Hungary, and Finland by the United States and Great Britain; the assessment of reparations from Germany and its allies; disposition of the German fleet; and setting the boundaries of Germany and Poland. Although Truman seemed uneasy about how he would get along with the sometimes difficult Churchill, he was more concerned about dealing with Stalin. He hoped that the atomic bomb would enhance his ability (and no doubt his self-confidence) in negotiating over issues at Potsdam, though he did not specify exactly how he thought the bomb would improve his leverage or how he might wield it if he had the opportunity. In Truman's mind, the primary American objective was to secure a firm pledge from Stalin

FIGURE 4 President Harry S. Truman conferring with James F. Byrnes (left) and
William D. Leahy aboard the USS *Augusta* on the way to Potsdam, July 1945.
(U.S. Navy, courtesy Harry S. Truman Library)

about the timing of Soviet entry into the war against Japan; apparently
he had concluded that the bomb would make his negotiations with Stalin
over this issue easier.

As Truman sailed across the Atlantic Ocean on his way to Potsdam,
General Groves and the scientists at Los Alamos were working at a furi-
ous pace to complete preparations for the test of the plutonium bomb.
The timing was not coincidental; although Stalin and Churchill had
pleaded for an earlier date, the president had deliberately postponed
the Potsdam meeting to mid-July 1945, after the test of the bomb was
scheduled to take place. Despite the best efforts of the scientists and
technicians at Los Alamos, who were preparing the test site in the desert
near Alamogordo, New Mexico, and completing final experiments on
the implosion design, the deadline had to be pushed back. Oppenheimer
later recalled that he and his colleagues "were under incredible pressure

to get it done before the Potsdam meeting." The first date that the scientists could be ready was July 16, and some thought a later time would be more suitable. But Groves strongly resisted any further postponement, because, he said, the "upper crust" insisted on a test "as soon as possible." It was not clear precisely who made up the "upper crust" that Groves cited as his "higher authority," but it was clear that Truman and his advisers wanted assurance of a successful atomic test in time for the Potsdam meeting, which was scheduled to begin on July 16.[3]

Final preparations for the atomic test, which Oppenheimer had given the name "Trinity," proceeded amid strain, excitement, uncertainty, and ominous weather forecasts. Work at the site, located about 200 miles from Los Alamos, had proceeded in earnest since May 1945, as shelters were built, electrical wiring strung, telephone lines connected, and scientific instruments installed. The most obvious feature at the site was a 100-foot-tall steel tower at ground zero, where the bomb would be placed before it was detonated. Most of the observers of the test would watch from a hill about 20 miles away or the base camp about 10 miles away, though a few would huddle in shelters about five miles from the tower. In the last hours before the shot, which was scheduled for 4:00 A.M. on July 16, tensions escalated—over the approaching culmination of years of effort on nuclear fission and the implosion design, over a last-minute experiment that seemed to indicate that the test was doomed to fail, and especially over a ferocious thunderstorm that started about 2:00 A.M. on the morning of the test. "It was raining cats and dogs, lightning and thunder," one scientist recalled. "[We were] really scared [that] this object there in the tower might be set off accidentally."[4]

Groves, after learning from the camp's meteorologist that the storm would let up by dawn and threatening to hang him if he was wrong, rescheduled the shot for 5:30 A.M. The countdown proceeded without a hitch, and the bomb exploded with a stupendous production of light, heat, and noise. Some observers were most impressed by the dazzling light; one recalled that "we saw the whole sky flash with unbelievable brightness in spite of the very dark glasses we wore." Others remembered the heat more vividly. Even 10 miles from ground zero, physicist Philip Morrison recounted, "the thing that got me was not the flash but the blinding heat of a bright day on your face in the cold desert morning." The rumble of noise from the blast rolled through the area for a full five minutes; it sounded to test participants as though a train were rushing by within easy reach.[5] The reaction of the scientists and soldiers at

FIGURE 5 Test explosion of atomic bomb, Alamogordo, New Mexico, July 16, 1945. (Los Alamos Scientific Laboratory, courtesy Harry S. Truman Library)

Alamogordo was a mixture of awe, elation, and relief, which in some cases was promptly followed by a sense of profound concern about what would be done with the new force they had witnessed.

At 8:00 A.M., Groves reported the successful test to Stimson's aide George Harrison in Washington, and an hour later called to add a few more details. Harrison sent a cryptic message to Stimson at Potsdam, informing him in coded language of the results of the test: "Operated on this morning. Diagnosis not yet complete but results seem satisfactory and already exceed expectations." Stimson received the message at 7:30 P.M. and took it immediately to Truman and Byrnes. They were, he noted in his diary, "delighted with it."⁶ The arrival of the news about the successful atomic test came just before the start of the conference, which had been postponed for a day because Stalin was ill and had arrived late.

On July 17, the president met his Soviet counterpart for the first time. Stalin called on Truman close to noontime, and they talked frankly over lunch for about two hours. The president noted in his diary after the discussion that he could "deal with Stalin," who was, he wrote, "honest—but smart as hell." Stalin had revealed some "dynamite" by setting out his views on the questions of Franco, Italian colonies, and Chinese concessions, but the president noted that "I have some dynamite too which I'm not exploding right now." Most importantly to Truman, Stalin pledged that he would "be in the Jap War on August 15th." The president reacted to this news by commenting: "Fini Japs when that comes about."[7]

Truman's diary notes, jotted shortly after his conversation with Stalin, reflect the euphoria he must have felt. His discussions with Stalin had gone well, and he seemed confident that he could get along with the Soviet leader. He was elated that he had achieved his primary objective without enduring difficult negotiations or making concessions. Stalin's promise that he would enter the war with Japan on August 15 gave the president exactly what he wanted—a reaffirmation of Soviet intentions to enter the Pacific war and a firm date by which they would do it. His satisfaction was clear in a letter he wrote to Mrs. Truman on July 18: "I've gotten what I came for—Stalin goes to war August 15 with no strings on it. . . . I'll say we'll end the war a year sooner now, and think of the kids who won't get killed. That is the important thing."[8]

The meaning of Truman's exclamation in his diary that Soviet participation in the war would "Fini Japs" is less clear. Some scholars have suggested that Truman's statement shows he felt certain that Soviet entry would end the war without an invasion or without the use of the atomic bomb.[9] But this is doubtful. Truman's advisers had not told him that a Soviet declaration of war on Japan would force a surrender by itself, so his notation did not represent their assessment. The president knew that the Trinity test had succeeded by the time he met Stalin, as his mention of his "dynamite" demonstrated, though he knew little about how powerful the test explosion had been. His "Fini Japs" comment appears to have been linked to the reference to his "dynamite," suggesting that he thought the atomic bomb and Soviet entry together would finish the Japanese. He placed no time frame on his "Fini Japs" remark. Presumably he believed that Japan would quit the war fairly soon after the Soviets invaded Manchuria, but this would not satisfy his desire for a surrender at the earliest possible moment.

Although Truman's diary notations, in this case and in others, provide important clues to his thinking, they often recorded his mood more accurately than they did reports or evaluations he received from his advisers. Thus, "Fini Japs" indicated the president's jubilation over the success of his first talk with Stalin and his relief over achieving his primary objective so effortlessly. It did not, however, reflect a considered summary of the views of American leaders about the end of the war or a conviction on the part of the president that the war would end on August 15 when the Soviets invaded Manchuria or shortly thereafter.

The news about the success of the Trinity test gave Truman greater self-assurance in dealing with Churchill and Stalin. He displayed his increased confidence in the first plenary sessions of the conference. On July 18, he wrote to Mrs. Truman that at the previous day's meeting he "gave them an earful." Two days later he reported a "tough meeting" on July 19 at which "I reared up my hind legs and told 'em where to get off and they got off." Truman no longer recited the doubts and anxieties he had expressed before the conference began, though he exaggerated his dominance of the meetings in his letters to his wife. The major disputes took place between Churchill and Stalin, and according to the official minutes of the sessions, Truman had comparatively little to say. He continued to focus on his desire to end the Pacific war, with the assistance of both Great Britain and the Soviet Union, as rapidly as possible. Having achieved his major objective of securing Stalin's pledge to join the war against Japan, he seemed to take only limited interest in the European questions on the agenda.[10]

Truman received further information about the Trinity test on the morning of July 18. Another coded message from Washington told Stimson that light from the explosion could be seen for 250 miles and its roar heard 50 miles from the site. The secretary of war promptly informed the president, who was gratified to learn about the bomb's tremendous power. On July 21, a courier handed the first detailed report from Groves about the Trinity test to Stimson. The secretary of war called it "an immensely powerful document."[11] Groves disclosed that the "test was successful beyond the most optimistic expectations of anyone.... I estimate the energy generated to be in excess of the equivalent of 15,000 to 20,000 tons of TNT; and this is a conservative estimate." Groves's account of the power of the explosion was uncharacteristically effusive. He also enclosed comments of General Thomas F. Farrell, who had witnessed the test from one of the closest vantage points and who eloquently described what he had seen: "The effects could well be called unprecedented, magnificent, beautiful, stupendous, and terrifying. . . . The whole country was lighted by a searing light with the intensity many times that of the midday sun. It was golden, purple, violet, gray, and blue. It lighted every peak, crevasse, and ridge of the nearby mountain range with a clarity and beauty that cannot be described but must be seen to be imagined. It was that beauty the great poets dream about but describe most poorly and inadequately." Farrell observed that the "great new force" could be "used for good or for evil."[12] Stimson read Groves's report in its entirety to Byrnes and Truman; they were "immensely pleased." The president remarked that "it gave him an entirely new feeling of confidence."[13]

As the Potsdam meeting continued, Truman's views of the bomb became more ambivalent. At first he was unambiguously delighted with the news of the successful test. On July 18, after receiving the second report on the bomb and the first indication of its power, he recorded in his diary his certainty that the bomb ensured the war would end soon. "Believe Japs will fold up before Russia comes in," he wrote. "I am sure they will when Manhattan appears over their homeland." A week later, in Truman's next entry about the bomb, he was more reflective and more reserved about its implications. "We have discovered the most terrible bomb in the history of the world," he observed. "It may be the fire destruction prophesied in the Euphrates Valley Era, after Noah and his fabulous Ark." The president thought that it was "certainly a good thing for the world that Hitler's crowd or Stalin's did not discover this atomic bomb," and added: "It seems to be the most terrible thing ever discovered, but it can be made the most useful."[14]

Truman's recognition that the atomic bomb was something qualitatively different from other weapons of war and that its destructive power made it the "most terrible thing ever discovered" did not move him to call a meeting with his most trusted advisers to discuss it. He did not ask for position papers on the advantages and disadvantages of using, or not using, the new weapon. He did not seek advice on its potential impact on forcing a quick Japanese surrender or on affecting the postwar world. He did not request staff studies on whether the bomb would be, on balance, a favorable or unfavorable development in the military and diplomatic position of the United States.

Truman remained primarily concerned with ending the war as soon as possible, and the bomb was the most likely and least risky means to accomplish his objective. Therefore, discussions with his advisers about its use, even if it was "the most terrible bomb in the history of the world," hardly seemed necessary. The use of the bomb was not entirely a foregone conclusion; Truman could have decided against it. But he had no compelling reason to do so. The bomb provided a promising way to bring about a prompt Japanese surrender without the disadvantages of other alternatives, and in Truman's mind, its use did not require lengthy consideration.

In keeping with the assumption of Truman and his advisers that the bomb would be used when ready, the president did not issue an order to drop it on Japan. There is no single document that shows Truman's decision to use the bomb. There were two military orders that instructed the Army Air Forces to deliver the bomb on Japanese cities, both of which resulted from informal discussions between Groves and other Army leaders over a period of a week. General Carl A. Spaatz, commander of the strategic air forces in the Pacific and Arnold's chief lieutenant, insisted on a formal order to drop the bomb. On July 24, General Arnold received an order, the authority for which was unstated, to drop the uranium 235, gun-type bomb between August 1 and 10 on one of four Japanese cities—Hiroshima, Kokura, Niigata, or Nagasaki. The following day a clarifying order from Marshall's deputy, General Thomas T. Handy, called for delivery of the first bomb as soon as weather permitted "after about 3 August 1945." It also directed that "additional bombs will be delivered . . . as soon as made ready by the project staff." This order was sent "by direction and with the approval of" Stimson and Marshall.[15]

Stimson talked with Truman on July 24 and informed him about the proposed targets and dates for the use of the bomb. He also made a special appeal that the ancient Japanese capital of Kyoto, a center of culture and learning, be spared from an atomic attack. Stimson had taken this position for weeks against the resistance of Groves and other military officials, and Truman reiterated his concurrence with the secretary of war. The following day the president, recording his recollection of the conversation, stated that he told Stimson to use the bomb "so that military objectives and soldiers and sailors are the target and not women and children." Truman also noted: "He and I are in accord. The target will be a purely military one."[16] The source of this comment is not clear. Stimson did not mention any conversation about the target being "a purely military one" in his diary. He knew better; he had been deeply troubled about the deaths and injuries among noncombatants caused by the bombing of Japan with conventional weapons, and he harbored no illusions that the effects of the new bomb would be limited to military installations.

It was apparent that the targeted cities were not primarily military bases and that the atomic bomb would kill many women and children as well as soldiers and sailors. Hiroshima, which topped the list, had a population of about 350,000 and was a regional headquarters for the Japanese army. But it was not a vital military target; if it had been, it would have been bombed in earlier B-29 raids. The city had been spared from conventional bombing in order to allow a more dramatic demonstration of the destructive power of the atomic bomb. American leaders valued the bomb for its potential shock effect on the Japanese population and government. The atomic attack on Hiroshima would not be confined to military targets any more than the firebombings of other cities had been. Truman's diary notation is attributable, as historian Barton J. Bernstein has suggested, only to "self-deception."[17]

Although the reports on the enormous power of the plutonium bomb tested at Alamogordo did not lead to a reconsideration of its military consequences or its use against Japan, they did prompt an effort to take advantage of its potential diplomatic benefits. The central question surrounding the diplomatic impact of the bomb was its effect on U.S.-Soviet relations. The Trinity test brought this issue to a head. Stimson and the Interim Committee he had established had reflected on the impact of the bomb on postwar U.S.-Soviet diplomacy; they had reached different conclusions at different times about how and whether the United States should approach the Soviets with information about the Manhattan Project. Byrnes, by contrast, remained firmly committed to the belief that the bomb provided an instrument to advance American diplomatic goals, especially in addressing growing differences with the Soviet Union.

The details about the bomb's power, which reached Potsdam on July 21, made Truman more assertive in his discussions with Churchill and Stalin and more engaged in European issues. They also brought about a reversal of his objective of seeking a prompt Soviet entry into the war with Japan. Truman did not want to cause a rift in U.S.-Soviet relations, but he followed Byrnes's lead in acting on an ill-defined premise that the bomb would improve the U.S. position in negotiations with the Soviet Union. As Stimson noted in his diary on July 23, "The program for S1 [code name for the atomic bomb] is tying in what we are doing in all fields."[18]

An hour or so after Truman heard Groves's detailed account of the Trinity test from Stimson, he met with Churchill and Stalin at the fifth plenary session of the conference. The president played an active role in the discussions and took sharp exception to Stalin's positions on extending diplomatic recognition to Rumania, Bulgaria, Hungary, and

FIGURE 6 Winston Churchill, President Truman, and Joseph Stalin at Potsdam. (U.S. Army, courtesy Harry S. Truman Library)

Finland; elections in and the boundaries of Poland; and the economic rehabilitation of Germany. The following day, Stimson gave Churchill a copy of Groves's report on the Trinity test, and the prime minister remarked: "Now I know what happened to Truman yesterday. . . . When he got to the meeting after having read this report he was a changed man. He told the Russians just where they got on and off and generally bossed the whole meeting."[19]

Although the issues that Truman debated with Stalin would have caused differences of opinion under any circumstances, there is little question that the president's demeanor changed noticeably as a result of the news he received about the bomb test. He was more confident and more inclined to challenge Soviet claims. As the conference went on, Truman became more outspoken in complaining about Soviet intentions to expand their influence in Eastern Europe, Turkey, and the Mediterranean, about their position on reparations, and other issues. He told Stimson that he would resist Soviet demands, "apparently," the secretary of war noted, because he was "relying greatly upon the information as to S1."[20]

On the diplomatic front, Truman took his cue from Byrnes, who believed that the bomb offered the means to resist Soviet control of Eastern Europe and ambitions elsewhere. He was willing, and indeed eager, to postpone settlement of outstanding issues until after Potsdam— and after use of the atomic bomb against Japan. In contrast to military issues, which received consideration from many high-level presidential advisers, Byrnes exercised tight command over diplomatic questions. Truman largely deferred to his secretary of state, who was, in the phrase of historian Robert L. Messer, the "'assistant president' in charge of the peace."[21] In Byrnes's judgment, the use of the bomb would so impress the Soviets that his job of negotiating over matters not resolved at Potsdam would be made much easier. He told former American ambassador to the Soviet Union Joseph E. Davies that American possession of the bomb "would have some effect [on the Soviets] and induce them to yield and agree to our position." He suggested that "the New Mexico situation had given us great power, and that in the last analysis it would control."[22] Byrnes's view was not circulated to and deliberated over by other top American officials, and by his fiat it became the basis for policy for a time after the war. It did not, however, take precedence over military considerations in the use of the bomb against Japan.

As a result of the success of the Trinity test, Byrnes also took the lead in revising American views on the desirability of Soviet participation in the Pacific war. Truman had been delighted on the first day of the meeting that Stalin had promised to enter the war on August 15, and on July 20 he had told Mrs. Truman that he wanted the assistance of both the British and the Soviets in defeating Japan. As late as July 24 he had given his approval to a paper prepared by the British and American Combined Chiefs of Staff that, among other things, recommended that Soviet participation in the war be encouraged. After receiving the details about the atomic test, however, Byrnes, apparently on his own initiative, took a different position. He sought to prevent, or at least delay, Soviet entry into the war in order to diminish their influence in East Asia.

Byrnes encouraged the Chinese foreign minister, T. V. Soong, to prolong discussions he was conducting with the Soviets over promises Roosevelt had given Stalin at Yalta regarding concessions in China. Based on a statement Stalin made to Harry Hopkins in May 1945, indicating that he would not enter the Pacific war until the Chinese accepted the Yalta agreement, Byrnes hoped that if Soong extended the negotiations the Soviets would stay out of the war, at least for a time. He did this in spite of his own recognition that the Soviets would join the war for their own purposes no matter what the status of their negotiations with China.[23] Apparently the power of the atomic test emboldened Byrnes to try to delay Soviet entry. He commented that once the bomb was dropped, "Japan will surrender and Russia will not get in so much on the kill."[24] In his mind, the bomb offered a way to end the war while sharply reducing the unfavorable effects of Soviet participation.

Truman's top military advisers agreed that Soviet entry into the war was no longer essential or desirable. On July 22, the president asked Stimson whether Marshall "felt that we needed the Russians in the war or whether we could get along without them." When Stimson posed the question to Marshall, the general pointed out that Soviet troops were massing on the border of Manchuria. Even if the Japanese surrendered before Soviet entry into the war, he argued, "that would not prevent the Russians from marching into Manchuria anyhow and striking, thus permitting them to get virtually what they wanted."[25] Implicitly, Marshall took issue with Byrnes's ill-considered hope that the Soviets would hold off invading Manchuria simply because they had not yet reached an agreement with China.

In response to Stimson's question, Marshall suggested that the atomic bomb made Soviet entry into the war unnecessary for achieving victory over Japan. Stimson passed along this judgment to the president. Marshall himself told Truman in a memorandum of July 26 that he planned to leave the conference the following day because "military business" had been completed. Further, his departure would indicate "to the Russians that we were not in a position of soliciting their support nor dependent upon their participation in the war in the Far East."[26] Truman did not enunciate his own position, but there is no reason to think that he disagreed with his advisers. Late in the conference, when Stalin asked for a formal American request that the Soviet Union enter the

Pacific war, Truman sidestepped the issue. The effect of the conclusion that the United States did not require Soviet assistance on planning for the end of the war was inconsequential except to show that American policymakers at that point were persuaded that the bomb was likely to force a Japanese surrender without the shock of a Soviet declaration of war. They realized that Stalin would invade Manchuria as soon as possible, and they were not, in their view, sacrificing military objectives by backing off from their desire for Soviet entry into the war against Japan.

The position that Truman and Byrnes took on Soviet entry into the war was a clear sign of their growing concern over the expansion of Soviet power and their hope that the atomic bomb would serve as a forceful diplomatic weapon after the war. Nevertheless, Truman still wanted to get along with the Soviet Union and to find ways to settle differences. He had not reached a conclusion that the two nations were headed for an irreconcilable rift. He worried about Stalin's health and what would happen if a new leader took over in the Soviet Union. He told Mrs. Truman: "I like Stalin. He is straightforward. Knows what he wants and will compromise when he can't get it."[27] When the Soviet leader became ill one day toward the end of the conference, the president speculated about what would happen "if Stalin should suddenly cash in." His concern was that "if some demagogue on horseback gained control of the efficient Russian military machine he could play havoc with European peace for a while."[28]

In order to avoid offending the Soviets and aggravating discord, Truman decided that he must approach Stalin with information about the atomic bomb. He had received conflicting advice on whether or not to inform Stalin. Byrnes opposed it because he feared that the Soviets would ask to join an atomic partnership, or worse, from his perspective, rush to enter the war against Japan. Other American officials contended that a failure to disclose something to Stalin about the success of the atomic project and plans to use the bomb against Japan would create a great deal of bitterness and distrust toward the United States. Truman compromised between the differing arguments by electing to tell Stalin about the bomb in vague terms and in a way that would discourage questions or solicitation of additional information.

On July 24, after a plenary session, Truman strolled over to Stalin with an air of studied nonchalance and mentioned that the United States had developed a new weapon of "unusual destructive force." Stalin, according to Truman's memoirs, replied that he was pleased to hear of it and hoped that the president would make "good use of it against the Japanese."[29] Other witnesses, however, recalled that Stalin merely nodded his head or said, "Thank you." Byrnes and Churchill, who watched the conversation from a distance, were surprised and gratified that Stalin seemed to take so little interest in Truman's report. They concluded, incorrectly, that Stalin did not know what Truman was talking about.

Stalin knew perfectly well from Truman's oblique reference that his new weapon was an atomic bomb. The Soviets had undertaken their own effort to build the bomb in 1943, although it did not receive nearly the high-level support or the resources that were accorded the Manhattan Project. Stalin had not viewed the bomb as something that would be helpful in the war and therefore had given it only modest patronage. However, the Soviet project did benefit from espionage that transferred thousands of pages of secret information from the Manhattan Project and provided important assistance to Soviet scientists about the American approach to building a bomb. Although Stalin understood what Truman told him, he did not seem to grasp the enormous power of the atomic bomb or expect that the United States would have it available for use against Japan.

If Stalin had realized that the bomb could shorten the war, he would have been much more alarmed. He was deeply concerned that the Asian war would end before his troops invaded Manchuria. If that happened, he worried that the United States and Great Britain might not honor the promises they had made at Yalta in response to Soviet demands, including Soviet control of the port of Dairen, southern Sakhalin, and the Kurile Islands, joint operation of key railways with the Chinese government, and other concessions. Just before the Potsdam meeting opened, he had asked his military leaders whether Soviet entry into the war with Japan could be moved up to early August, but he was told they needed more time to prepare for the invasion. At the same time that Byrnes was trying to delay Soviet participation in the war in order to undermine Soviet claims in East Asia, Stalin was doing all he could to join the war to ensure that he received the concessions promised at Yalta. As Marshall realized, Stalin was anxious to declare war on Japan for his own reasons.[30]

As the conference wore on, Truman began to wear out. He tired of the seemingly endless negotiations, and his patience thinned as the meeting ran into its second week. Although he was proud of what was accomplished "in spite of all the talk," he longed to go home.[31] But important issues relating to the use of the atomic bomb and the end of the war with Japan remained to be addressed. Truman's advisers, in consultation with the British, worked hard to draft and then redraft press releases that the White House and the Pentagon would issue after the bomb was dropped. This was a matter of considerable importance; General Handy's order of July 25 that authorized the use of the bomb specified that "dissemination of any and all information concerning the use of the weapon against Japan is reserved to the Secretary of War and the President of the United States."[32]

Another question on which Truman sought advice was the effect of a sudden Japanese surrender on American society and economic well-being. Fred Vinson, who had appealed to the Joint Chiefs of Staff in May 1945 to ease the problems of conversion to a peacetime economy by reducing military demands on production, pressed Truman with the same arguments while the president was at Potsdam. In one cable he requested that the Joint Chiefs "make an immediate and thorough re-appraisal of all military requirements and of the strategic considerations upon which those requirements are based."[33]

The successful test of the atomic bomb apparently alerted Truman that the concerns Vinson cited might have to be addressed in the near future. The president asked Marshall for a report on, in the general's phrase, "the problem presented by Japanese capitulation in the near future." Marshall submitted his views on July 26; he suggested that the end of the war would not cause a major decline in industry or serious unemployment in the United States. He cautioned, however, that economic readjustment, military demobilization, and public acceptance of the need for some troops to remain overseas would "require a tremendous effort."[34]

The possibility that the bomb would bring about a sudden surrender also prompted military planners to consider arrangements for the occupation of Japan. On July 26, the Joint Chiefs sent a message to General MacArthur and Admiral Chester W. Nimitz, commander of U.S. naval forces in the Pacific, advising them that coordination of their plans for the procedures to be followed in the event of a Japanese surrender was a "pressing necessity." Another message from the Joint Chiefs told Mac-Arthur that Japanese capitulation could occur before the Soviets joined the war on August 15. Although the studies of and messages regarding an early surrender did not demonstrate that American policymakers felt certain the use of atomic bombs would end the war quickly, they did indicate that top officials hoped for that outcome and regarded it as a genuine possibility.[35]

The most important military issue that had to be resolved before the Potsdam Conference ended was the publication of a warning to Japan. After the June 18 meeting at which Truman approved the invasion of Kyushu, Stimson, Forrestal, and Grew had begun work on a statement that they hoped would induce a Japanese surrender "without a fight to the finish."[36] The secretary of war prepared a memorandum to the president, and on June 26, he and his two colleagues, the so-called "Committee of Three," agreed that although a warning to Japan might not bring about a surrender, "it might do so, and . . . no harm would result from trying." They also agreed that even if the Japanese did not respond favorably to the statement, "it might check in the U.S. a deterioration of will to complete the defeat of Japan, as it would make clear the necessity for fullest efforts if the Japanese did not accede."[37] The committee intended to offer the Japanese an opportunity to surrender but not an invitation to open negotiations on ending the war. On July 2, Stimson submitted to Truman his memorandum and a draft of a proposed proclamation from the United States, Great Britain, China, and possibly the Soviet Union. It was a strongly worded demand for the Japanese to quit the war, but it held out the possibility that "a constitutional monarchy under the present dynasty" might be retained.[38]

The draft became the basis for a warning to Japan that received further consideration and much revision at Potsdam. The key question was whether Japan should be given the opportunity to retain the imperial institution. Stimson, Marshall, Forrestal, Leahy, and Grew argued that the emperor should be allowed to remain, partly as an incentive for the Japanese to quit the war and partly because they thought he was the only person who could effectively order his troops to surrender. The Joint Chiefs made this point to the president on July 18: "From a strictly military point of view the Joint Chiefs of Staff consider it inadvisable to make any statement or take any action . . . that would make it difficult or impossible to utilize the authority of the Emperor to direct a surrender of the Japanese forces in the outlying areas as well as in Japan proper."[39] Alone among Truman's major advisers, Byrnes took a different view on modifying the policy of unconditional surrender to allow the retention of the emperor. The reasons for Byrnes's position are not entirely clear, but given his priorities, it is likely that he worried about the political consequences of changing a popular policy. He revised the draft of the declaration to eliminate any specific mention of allowing the emperor to remain. Truman's views on unconditional surrender are even more difficult to pin down. He might have gone along with Byrnes because he shared the same concerns. Or he might not have attached much importance to the proclamation because he doubted that Japan would respond favorably. The president noted in his diary on July 25: "We will issue a warning statement asking the Japs to surrender and save lives. I'm sure they will not do that, but we will have given them the chance."[40]

It seems most likely that Truman remained ambivalent about moderating unconditional surrender and, as a result, took no strong stand on it. On July 24, U.S. Navy Captain Ellis M. Zacharias made a radio address as a part of a series of broadcasts he delivered in a psychological warfare campaign. He offered Japan the possibility of surrendering according to the principles of the Atlantic Charter, which promised self-government to all nations. This indirectly suggested that the Japanese would be able to choose to keep the emperor. The Zacharias broadcast received a great deal of attention in newspapers in the United States and oblique expressions of interest from Japanese Foreign Minister Tōgō. It is unclear who, if anyone, authorized the position that Zacharias outlined, but it is clear that Truman made no effort to disavow it.[41] A few days later he also refrained from challenging Byrnes's revisions to a statement on modifying unconditional surrender that ran counter to Zacharias's comments and to the views of other high-level advisers. Rather than force the issue when he was uncertain about the best alternative and pessimistic about the chances that the proclamation would succeed, he seems to have allowed Byrnes to have his way by default.

The Potsdam Proclamation was issued on July 26 by the United States, Great Britain, and China. Byrnes opposed including the Soviet Union among the signatory powers, apparently because he was concerned that Stalin would ask for further concessions in East Asia in return for his signature. In keeping with its multiple authorship, the declaration was a hodgepodge of statements that reflected differing motives and concerns. It affirmed in unequivocal terms that Japan must throw off the rule of the military and establish a new order of peace: "The time has come for Japan to decide whether she will continue to be controlled by those self-willing militaristic advisers whose unintelligent calculations have brought the Empire of Japan to the threshold of annihilation, or whether she will follow the path of reason." The strong language was intended to avoid any suggestion to the Japanese that the Allied nations were inviting negotiations and to demonstrate to the American people that the government was not softening its position on a Japanese surrender.

Yet the declaration also held out the promise that the Japanese would be permitted to revive their national economy and would not "be enslaved as a race or destroyed as a nation." And, despite Byrnes's views, it left a slight opening for the retention of the emperor by calling for the unconditional surrender of the "Japanese armed forces" and for the establishment of a peaceful government formed by the "freely expressed will of the Japanese people." The proclamation did not inform the Japanese about the atomic bomb or the pending entry into the war of the Soviet army. It concluded by warning the Japanese that their alternatives were to agree to its terms for unconditional surrender or to face "prompt and utter destruction."[42]

The Potsdam Proclamation was not a clear exposition of American policy or intentions; its ambiguity demonstrated differing views and priorities among American policymakers. But it is doubtful that even a clear statement that offered Japan the opportunity to retain the imperial institution would have been acceptable to Japan and ended the war. The Japanese government remained paralyzed by its own deep divisions. Foreign Minister Tōgō recognized that the declaration, while using the phrase "unconditional surrender," in fact offered conditions that might lead to the end of the war. He wanted the government to withhold comment to prevent his opponents from flatly rejecting it. The die-hard military faction in the Supreme Council for the Direction of the War found the declaration offensive and unacceptable, but agreed to maintain silence for a time.

The Potsdam Proclamation soon confronted the Japanese government with a major problem. The Allies broadcast the text of the declaration to the Japanese people, and the Supreme Council, concerned about a loss of morale on the home front, decided that it must issue a statement. In doing so, it used a verb, *mokusatsu*, that could be translated as "ignore," "take no notice of," or "treat with silent contempt." In the context of the deliberations of the Supreme Council, it could conceivably have been translated to mean "withhold comment," but the grounds for this reading were not available to the American government.

Premier Suzuki, under growing pressure from the military to utterly reject the demands of the declaration, gave no reason to think that the Japanese were considering accepting it. He told a carefully staged press conference: "The government does not regard it as a thing of any great value. We will press forward to carry the war to a successful conclusion."[43] The U.S. government, therefore, could hardly have interpreted the Japanese response as anything but an outright and, indeed, contemptuous rejection of the terms of the Potsdam Proclamation. The implacable hostility of the military faction doomed any chance that the Japanese government would surrender on the basis of its provisions. Only decisive intervention by the emperor in favor of accepting the Potsdam Proclamation could have changed the Japanese position.

While Truman and his advisers were deliberating at Potsdam over ways to end the war, American soldiers were still fighting and dying. There were no major battlefronts after the capture of Okinawa, but the United States continued to sustain casualties in the Pacific theater. The numbers were not large compared to the costs of the Okinawa campaign or to the projected casualties for an invasion of Kyushu, but neither were they insignificant. In July 1945, the only full month between the end of the battle for Okinawa and the Japanese surrender, the U.S. Army, including the Army Air Forces, incurred a total of 1,332 casualties in the Pacific. Of those, 775 were killed in action. In addition, the Army suffered another 2,458 nonbattle deaths in July from accidents, disease, and other causes.[44]

There is no evidence that Truman received periodic reports on battle casualties from his advisers, and it is doubtful that he knew precisely how many American soldiers were being killed and wounded. But he was acutely aware that as long as the war went on, American soldiers and sailors would continue to die. He could look at a newspaper on any day and see casualty lists from earlier battles and photographs of young Americans who had lost their lives. The total of 3,233 deaths from all causes or 775 combat deaths in July were appreciable numbers that seem relatively small only if compared to higher losses in major battles and the projections for the invasion of Japan. The exact numbers were less important to the president than his commitment to ending American casualties by achieving victory as soon as possible. Truman was, after all, the World War I combat veteran who had "acted like a real baby" when one member of his unit died in France.

The costs of continuing the war were highlighted by the sinking of the cruiser USS *Indianapolis* on July 29, 1945. The *Indianapolis* had carried many of the components of the uranium 235 bomb to the island of Tinian, where they were assembled to make the atomic bomb later used against Hiroshima. After leaving Tinian, the ship was torpedoed by a

Japanese submarine and quickly sank. Hundreds of sailors were killed by the fires and explosions, but hundreds of others escaped the burning hulk. Many of them had reason to envy their slain brethren. For five days they floated unseen in the Pacific, suffering horrendously from exhaustion, sunburn, dehydration, heat, thirst, dementia, delirium, and stark terror. For some, the ordeal was cut short by marauding sharks, who attacked their helpless victims at will. Finally, the barely surviving crew members were spotted and rescued. As a result of the attack, the *Indianapolis* lost 880 of its crew of 1,196. The sinking of the *Indianapolis* occurred too late to have any impact on Truman's decision to use the atomic bomb. Nevertheless, it was a graphic illustration of what could happen as long as the war continued, even against an enemy that was teetering on the verge of defeat.[45]

The Potsdam Conference ended on August 2. As Truman had hoped, the successful test of the atomic bomb had played a major, if behind-the-scenes, role in the course of the meeting. But the president was uncertain or ambivalent about every important issue surrounding the military and diplomatic use of the new weapon except one. Although he was initially delighted with the news about Trinity, he soon became less exultant about the potential consequences of developing the atomic bomb. He largely deferred to Byrnes on the effort to delay Soviet entry into the war with Japan. He equivocated on informing Stalin about the bomb, and eventually sought middle ground by telling him about it in vague and uninformative terms. The president seemed unable to make up his mind on the question of modifying unconditional surrender and did not provide clear direction to his advisers. The one issue on which Truman was clear and decisive was that the bomb should be used against Japan to end the war at the earliest possible moment. It appeared to be the most likely way to force a prompt Japanese surrender without being burdened with the disadvantages of other options. For that reason, the use of the bomb was an easy and obvious military decision for Truman. The other questions the bomb presented were less immediate and considerably less important to him.

6

Hiroshima and Nagasaki

At 2:45 A.M. on August 6, 1945, a B-29 under the command of Colonel Paul W. Tibbets, a 29-year-old veteran pilot, began to roll down a runway on Tinian Island to take off on its historic mission to Hiroshima. The plane, which Tibbets had named *Enola Gay* after his mother, carried a crew of 12 men and an atomic bomb fueled with uranium 235. As it flew over Iwo Jima, it was joined by two other B-29s; their crews would seek scientific information on and take photographs of the blast. Tibbets informed his crew after takeoff that the cargo they would deliver was an atomic bomb, but otherwise the flight was uneventful. The weather was clear and the *Enola Gay* did not encounter resistance from anti-aircraft fire or enemy fighters. The fleet of just three planes caused little alarm when it appeared over Hiroshima; no warning sirens sounded and citizens saw no reason to seek shelter.

At about 8:15 A.M. (Hiroshima time) the *Enola Gay*'s bombardier released the bomb. It was festooned with messages that would never be read, some obscene, some wrathful; one offered "Greetings to the Emperor from the men of the *Indianapolis*." Forty-three seconds after leaving the plane, the bomb exploded, proving that the uranium 235, gun-type design worked as Manhattan Project scientists had promised. Even at 30,000 feet and 11 miles from ground zero, the Enola Gay was hit by two strong shock waves that bounced it around in the air and made a noise, as one crew member recalled, "like a piece of sheet metal snapping." When the plane circled back to take a look at the effects of the atomic bomb, even the battle-hardened veterans aboard were stunned. Copilot Robert Lewis declared: "We were struck dumb at the sight. It far exceeded all our expectations. Even though we expected something terrific, the actual sight caused all of us to feel that we were Buck Rogers 25th Century Warriors." Tail gunner Robert Caron described the mushroom cloud from the explosion as "a spectacular sight, a bubbling mass of purple-gray smoke."[1]

On the ground the bomb produced a ghastly scene of ruin, desolation, and human suffering. After the bomb exploded in the air about 1,900 feet above Hiroshima, witnesses reported seeing a searing flash of light, feeling a sweeping rush of air, and hearing a deafening roar, which was intensified by the sound of collapsing buildings. The city lay on flat ground on the edge of Hiroshima Bay, and the level surface on which it was situated allowed the destructive energy of the atomic bomb to flow evenly outward from the point of detonation. As a result, an area of about 4.4 square miles surrounding ground zero was almost

FIGURE 7 Hiroshima after the atomic attack. (National Archives 306-PS-B-49–5295)

completely devastated. Only a few structures that had been built to withstand earthquakes were strong enough to weather the atomic blast.

The bomb created what one survivor called "the hell I had always read about." Within a radius of a half mile or so, the force of the blast killed virtually everybody instantaneously. Farther away from ground zero, the effects were somewhat less lethal but still altogether terrible. The bomb gave off a flash of intense heat that not only caused many deaths and severe injuries but also helped to form a huge and all-consuming firestorm. The survivors of the blast and heat were often horribly debilitated. Blinded by the flash, burned and blistered by the heat, cut beyond recognition by flying glass, those who could move stumbled through the darkness caused by dust, smoke, and debris. It was common to see people whose skin was hanging off their bodies, a result of the thermal flash and the heat, which together caused severe blistering and tearing of the skin. Charred corpses were everywhere, and no services were available to help the living put out fires, salve their wounds, and ease their agony.

The survivors were often so weakened that they died from their injuries or from the later effects of radiation, which began to show up within a few days of the attack.[2]

President Truman received two sketchy reports about the success of the atomic bomb aboard the cruiser USS *Augusta* as he sailed home from Potsdam. Elated by the news, he remarked to a group of sailors, "This is the greatest thing in history." A few minutes later he told the cheering crew of the ship about the power of the bomb. Truman's expectation that the bomb would bring the war to a prompt finish made him jubilant and, for the moment at least, superseded the ambivalence he had privately expressed at Potsdam about the development of nuclear weapons.[3]

Within a short time the White House released a statement from the president about the atomic bomb. It revealed that the bomb "had more power than 20,000 tons of T.N.T." and commented that the Japanese had "been repaid many fold" for their attack on Pearl Harbor. The president threatened that if Japan failed to surrender quickly, it would suffer more atomic attacks: "We are now prepared to obliterate more rapidly and completely every productive enterprise the Japanese have above ground in any city. . . . If [their leaders] do not now accept our terms they may expect a rain of ruin from the air, the like of which has never been seen on this earth." The statement sought to take advantage of the shock of the first bomb by suggesting that the United States had a stockpile of atomic weapons that soon would be used against Japan. In fact, it had only one more atomic bomb that would be available within a short time.[4] To reinforce the shock value of the bomb, American forces in the Pacific hastily prepared 6 million leaflets to drop on Japanese cities. The leaflets informed their readers that Hiroshima had been destroyed by an atomic bomb and appealed to them to press their leaders for peace. They also urged Japanese citizens to evacuate cities in order to avoid exposure to further atomic attacks.[5]

While the leaflets were being prepared, an assembly team was rushing to ready the second bomb for delivery to Japan. The date for the attack was originally August 11, but discouraging weather forecasts pushed the schedule ahead by two days. On August 9, a B-29 named *Bock's Car* after its usual commander but piloted on this occasion by Major Charles W. Sweeney took off from Tinian. It carried a plutonium bomb of the same design as that tested at Alamogordo. Its primary target was the Japanese city of Kokura. The flight of *Bock's Car* was much more harrowing than that of the *Enola Gay* three days earlier. After enduring stormy weather and enemy flak, the plane was unable to drop its bomb on Kokura because of a heavy haze. With fuel running low, it headed for its secondary target, Nagasaki. Nagasaki was covered by clouds, but as the plane approached, the cloud cover opened slightly to give the bombardier a brief view of the city. Unable to find the planned target point, he used a stadium as a landmark to guide his aim.

Nagasaki was a densely populated industrial city in western Kyushu. At one time it had been a bustling port, but it had declined in importance as a commercial center. The city's economy depended heavily on the Mitsubishi Corporation, which operated shipyards, electrical equipment works, steel mills, and an arms plant that together employed 90 percent of Nagasaki's workforce. Although the city had not entirely escaped bombing by American air forces in previous months, it was relatively intact.

Because of the hills that rise above Nagasaki, the effects of the bomb were less widespread than in Hiroshima, but they were more intense in areas close to ground zero. The bomb destroyed a hospital and medical school that lay within 3,000 feet of the explosion and seriously damaged the Mitsubishi electrical equipment, steel, and arms factories. Within a radius of a half-mile or so, humans and animals died instantly, as in Hiroshima. The survivors also suffered the effects of injuries, radiation exposure, shock, helplessness, and fear that the residents of Hiroshima had experienced three days earlier. Nagasaki was fortunate to be spared from a raging firestorm, but the consequences of the atomic attack were still, by any standard, dreadful. Ironically, it was not until the day after the second bomb was used that leaflets prepared after Hiroshima that warned Japanese citizens about further atomic attacks were dropped on Nagasaki.[6]

It is impossible to measure accurately how many people in Hiroshima and Nagasaki were killed by the atomic bombs. The United States Strategic Bombing Survey, which conducted a thorough study of the effects of the bombs shortly after the war, estimated the number of deaths in Hiroshima at between 70,000 and 80,000 in a population of about 350,000 and in Nagasaki at about 35,000 in a population of about 270,000. More recent analyses have raised the mortality figures to about 166,000 in Hiroshima and between 60,000 and 80,000 in Nagasaki by the beginning of December 1945. The enormity of the death and destruction caused by the single bombs dropped on Hiroshima and Nagasaki was one major difference in their effects from those of the aerial attacks on Japanese cities with conventional weapons.

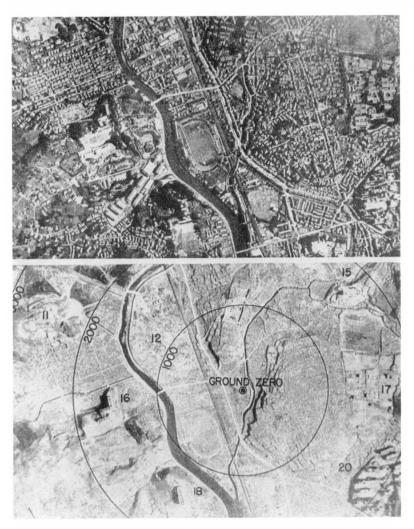

FIGURE 8 Nagasaki before and after being hit with the atomic bomb.
(National Archives 77-MHD-12.3)

The other important distinction in the use of atomic bombs was the death and illness that residents of the two cities suffered from ionizing radiation. The report of the Strategic Bombing Survey suggested that 15–20 percent of the fatalities in the first few weeks after the bombs fell were the result of acute exposure to radiation. It also found "reason to believe" that even if the effects of blast and heat had not been present, "the number of deaths among people within a radius of one-half mile from ground zero would have been almost as great as the actual figures and the deaths among those within 1 mile would have been only slightly less." The lethal levels of "initial radiation" came from the process of nuclear fission that fueled the bombs. The explosions released large inventories of radioactive "fission products" to the environment. The dose of radiation an individual received and the damage it caused depended on distance from the hypocenter (directly below the atmospheric explosions) and other variables such as shielding from buildings or topographical features and the position of the body relative to the path the radiation traveled. Although the death toll from nearly instantaneous exposure to initial radiation from the bombs cannot be calculated with precision, it clearly was a large number.

Levels of "residual radiation" from atmospheric fallout and deposits in the soil and building materials were less harmful than exposure to initial radiation by orders of magnitude. Nevertheless, they were a source of concern because of their potential long-term health effects on survivors of the atomic attacks. Both of the bombs were air bursts that went off several hundred feet above the ground (about 1,900 feet at Hiroshima and about 1,600 feet at Nagasaki). This greatly reduced the radioactive fallout they produced, though limited quantities of radioactive particles were dispersed in the atmosphere and slowly descended to earth. Survivors in Hiroshima and Nagasaki feared that "black rain" that fell on their cities was an indication of high levels of fallout. In fact, the black rain was caused by soot from the fires that raged on the ground and was not related to radiation releases from the bombs.

The exposures from residual radiation were generally far lower than from initial radiation, but they have been blamed for causing a massive number of deaths from cancer over the years. Historian Paul Ham, for example, claimed in 2014 that "hundreds of thousands" of survivors of the atomic explosions have "succumbed to cancers linked to radiation poisoning." Careful studies conducted by American and Japanese scientists on the health effects of radiation in Hiroshima and Nagasaki since 1948 tell a quite different story. The Radiation Effects Research Foundation, by tracing the health histories of a cohort of about 94,000 atomic bomb survivors, has calculated the number of "excess deaths" above the normal incidence of cancer mortality in the two cities. Its most recent report estimated the number of excess deaths from slow-developing solid tumors between 1958 and 1998 to have been 848. It estimated the number of excess deaths from leukemia, which shows up more quickly, between 1950 and 2000 to have been 94. The foundation concluded that the number of radiation-induced cancer deaths over a period of several decades was about 940. It assumed that the cohort on which it based its findings represented about one-half of the atomic bomb survivors in Hiroshima and Nagasaki, so it doubled its estimates to yield a total of about 1,900 excess deaths from cancer. This is a serious number that should not be taken lightly, but it is far short of epidemic proportions.[7]

In August 1945, the effects of radiation were much less of a concern than the impact of the atomic bomb on the Pacific war and international politics. The power of the bombs used against Japan and the story behind their development were featured in prominent headlines and in column after column of newsprint in the United States. Press treatment of the news generally reflected the tone of gratitude, pride, and confidence that the war would soon end that Truman and other American officials presented. But in some press accounts there was also a trace of uneasiness about the long-term consequences of the atomic bomb. As popular radio commentator H. V. Kaltenborn put it in a broadcast on the evening of August 6: "For all we know we have created a Frankenstein! We must assume that with the passage of only a little time, an improved form of the new weapon we use today can be turned against us."[8]

In Moscow, Joseph Stalin was concerned that the bomb would be turned against him, at least politically. After receiving the news about Hiroshima, he became intensely concerned that the bomb would deprive him of his objectives in Asia. He immediately ordered Soviet troops to attack Manchuria. Stalin did not wait for an agreement with China but hastened to join the Pacific war out of fear that the Japanese would surrender. On August 8, Soviet Foreign Minister Molotov informed Ambassador Satō that his country would consider itself at war with Japan the following day. Hours later, 1.5 million Soviet troops launched the invasion. They quickly routed the inferior Japanese forces, who surrendered in droves.

Stalin also established a new committee to make the atomic project a top priority and speed progress in constructing a Soviet bomb. Stalin viewed Truman's use of the bomb as a political act intended to deny him the gains he had been promised in Asia. He also regarded the bomb as a serious threat to the long-term international position of the Soviet Union by distorting the balance of power. "Hiroshima has shaken the whole world," he reportedly remarked. "The balance has been destroyed."[9]

In Tokyo, Japanese leaders were slower to recognize, or to acknowledge, the new force with which they had to deal. They did not receive details about the destruction of Hiroshima for several hours because of the loss of communications in the devastated city. The awful truth came in a report early in the morning of August 7: "The whole city of Hiroshima was destroyed instantly by a single bomb."[10] Within a short time, Japanese officials also learned of Truman's statement threatening a "rain of ruin" and announcing that Hiroshima had been attacked by an atomic bomb. They responded by sending a team of experts to Hiroshima to investigate the damage. The die-hard military faction insisted that Truman's announcement was mere propaganda and that the weapon used against Hiroshima was not an atomic bomb.

The emperor was deeply disturbed upon learning on the morning of August 7 that the United States had razed Hiroshima with an atomic weapon. Later in the day he pressed Lord Keeper of the Privy Seal Kido, his closest adviser, for further information about the bomb. The next morning he told Foreign Minister Tōgō: "Now that such a new weapon has appeared, it has become less and less possible to continue the war.... So my wish is to make such arrangements as to end the war as soon as possible." The use of the bomb shocked Hirohito and finally overcame his ambivalence about the need to end the war expeditiously. But even the distressing news of the atomic attack was not enough to convince him to surrender immediately on the basis of the Potsdam Proclamation. Hirohito and other Japanese leaders continued to deliberate over the terms that they would find acceptable for quitting the war.

At the request of the emperor, Prime Minister Suzuki called a meeting of the Supreme Council for the Direction of the War for August 9. Before the meeting took place, the Japanese government received word that the disaster of Hiroshima was compounded by the Soviet Union's declaration of war. The Soviets had been massing troops and supplies on the Manchurian border for months; Stalin commented at Yalta that he "believed Japan realized Russia was coming into the war because they could see Russian troops on [the] border." Nevertheless, the Soviet invasion came as a stunning blow to many Japanese military and political leaders. Some of them still harbored the illusion that the Soviet Union would remain neutral or even mediate a peace settlement on more favorable terms than the Potsdam Proclamation offered. The Japanese army acted on the premise that the Soviets would not launch an attack on Manchuria before early 1946. Those ill-founded hopes were shattered by the Soviet offensive. The closure of the Soviet option suddenly made the Potsdam Proclamation much more appealing as the best means to end the war and retain the emperor.[11]

The dual jolts of the atomic bomb and the Soviet attack pushed the Japanese government toward surrender, but it reached a decision only after painful deliberations and acute internal controversy. When the Supreme Council for the Direction of the War met on the morning of August 9, Suzuki opened the discussion by arguing that Japan had no choice but to accept the Potsdam Proclamation with the sole condition that the imperial institution be preserved. War Minister Anami, Army Chief of Staff Umezu, and Navy Chief of Staff Toyoda sharply disagreed. They contended that Japan should insist not only that the emperor be retained but also that other conditions be admitted. They wanted the United States and its allies to greatly restrict or forgo entirely the occupation of Japan, permit the Japanese to conduct their own war trials, and allow the Japanese to disarm themselves. Foreign Minister Tōgō responded, quite accurately, that the only concession that had a chance of acceptance by the Allies was the retention of the emperor. He was certain that the other conditions would be flatly rejected. The members of the Supreme Council angrily debated those points without reaching a consensus. They were hopelessly deadlocked, with Suzuki, Tōgō, and Navy Minister Yonai lined up against Anami, Umezu, and Toyoda.

As the Supreme Council for the Direction of the War battled over the issue of surrender, it received the shocking news that Nagasaki had been hit with an atomic bomb. This demolished the argument of the diehards, who had dismissed the reality that the bomb that destroyed Hiroshima was an atomic explosive and the possibility that the United States had more weapons of equal power. The attack on Nagasaki showed not only that the United States had succeeded in developing an atomic bomb but also that it had built more than one. It also fed the fears of the peace faction that many more atomic bombs would be used against Japan. Its members maintained that the only way to preserve Japan's national polity was to surrender with the assurance that the emperor would not be removed. Kido worried about a popular uprising against the government if the war continued much longer.[12]

Despite the impact of the news about Nagasaki, the stalemate within the Supreme Council continued. Three members favored acceptance of the Potsdam Proclamation if the emperor were allowed to remain, while the other three demanded further conditions and called for all-out resistance if the Allies refused. The debate then moved from the Supreme

Council to the larger cabinet (of which Umezu and Toyoda were not members). It voted overwhelmingly against the militants' position by a margin of 13 to 3, but it required unanimity to act.

At that point, several former high-ranking Japanese government officials prevailed on Kido to persuade the emperor to intervene in support of Tōgō's argument. This was not an easy task. Hirohito apparently concurred with those who insisted on four conditions, and Kido was reluctant to challenge this position. But eventually he persuaded the emperor that the best way to preserve the national polity was to offer to accept the Potsdam Proclamation with one condition. Kido later explained that he "felt the situation was utterly hopeless," and he told Hirohito that "there was no alternative left" but to "have the government at once accept the Potsdam Declaration and bring the war to a close." The emperor's primary concern was saving himself and the imperial dynasty; shaken by the atomic attacks, the Soviet invasion, and the growing indications of popular discontent with his rule, he concluded that the Potsdam Proclamation was more palatable than the looming threat of Soviet expansion. Therefore, he agreed to address the cabinet and the Supreme Council, which was a major departure from standard procedures. Under normal conditions the emperor did not take an active role in deliberations but waited for his advisers to agree on a position. The "imperial conference" began close to midnight on August 9. After the opposing sides stated their views, Hirohito told his ministers that the time had come to "bear the unbearable." He announced his support for accepting the Potsdam Proclamation with the single condition of preservation of the imperial institution.[13]

Hirohito's comments were an expression of his will and not an order or binding decision, but they broke the deadlock. The Supreme Council and the cabinet agreed to his wish to offer to surrender. Even the diehards went along, partly out of respect for the emperor and partly because the atomic bomb, ironically, enabled them to save face. They could claim that the war was lost and surrender made necessary because of the enemy's scientific prowess in developing nuclear weapons rather than because of their own mistakes or miscalculations.[14]

On August 10, the Japanese government transmitted a message through the Swiss embassy to the United States (though it arrived first in Washington through a MAGIC intercept). It offered to accept the terms of the Potsdam Proclamation "with the understanding that the said declaration does not comprise any demand which prejudices the prerogatives of His

Majesty as a Sovereign Ruler."[15] The Japanese overture, welcome as it was, generated a spirited debate among Truman's advisers. Stimson, Forrestal, and Leahy, consistent with their earlier support for modifying unconditional surrender, urged that the United States agree to the proposal.

The Japanese offer largely set aside two of the disadvantages of softening unconditional surrender that had previously troubled American policymakers. If the United States had first approached Japan with more moderate terms, it might have encouraged and enhanced the credibility of the Japanese die-hard faction. But the fact that the initiative came from Japan indicated that the militants were willing to surrender on the basis of agreement to the single condition. An American proposal to mitigate surrender demands would also have run the risk of undermining morale and support for the war effort at home. But the Japanese provided what appeared to most high-level U.S. officials to be a sensible and painless way to end the war, especially since the retention of the emperor would greatly ease the potential difficulties of enforcing the surrender terms.

The lone holdout on accepting the Japanese proposal among Truman's key advisers was Byrnes. In part, he was troubled by objections raised by Japan experts in the State Department. They pointed out that the wording of the Japanese overture could leave the emperor on the throne with his powers undiminished. They convinced Byrnes that approving the conditional surrender offer was incompatible with the fundamental American war aim of eliminating Japan's ability to make war. Byrnes was probably even more concerned about the other potential drawback of backing off from unconditional surrender—it was politically risky. There was considerable evidence of strong popular support for insisting on unconditional surrender and removing Hirohito from his throne after the Japanese peace proposal became public knowledge. A Gallup poll on August 10, for example, showed that by a margin of almost two to one those surveyed wanted the United States to reject Japan's initiative. Byrnes remarked that agreeing to the Japanese terms could lead to the "crucifixion of [the] President."[16]

Byrnes's priorities were clear; he was more worried about the political consequences of softening unconditional surrender than about prolonging the war and allowing the Soviets to make greater gains in Asia. Truman shared Byrnes's political concerns, and as a result, he continued to equivocate on the question of the status of the emperor. Rather than choosing between the two positions, he asked Byrnes to draft a reply

to Japan's advantage." Without apologizing for Japan's aggression or mentioning the word "surrender," he went on to state that "the enemy has begun to employ a new and most cruel bomb, the power of which to do damage is indeed incalculable, taking the toll of many innocent lives." If the war continued, he said, "it would not only result in an ultimate collapse and obliteration of the Japanese nation, but also it would lead to the total extinction of human civilization."[22]

The combined shocks of the atomic attack on Hiroshima and the Soviet offensive in Manchuria were decisive in ending the Pacific war. In the words of Navy Minister Yonai, who favored surrender on the single condition that the imperial institution be retained, the atomic bomb and the Soviet invasion were "gifts from the gods" that brought the war to a prompt conclusion. After Hiroshima, the emperor for the first time came out unequivocally for surrender, and after Soviet entry into the war, he decided, after considerable hesitation, that he supported acceptance of the Potsdam Proclamation if the imperial dynasty were not abolished. The bombing of Hiroshima and the Soviet attack also had the salutary effect of greatly increasing the concern of Hirohito and his top advisers that growing popular dissatisfaction with the government represented a genuine threat to the imperial system.

Although the dual shocks of the atomic bomb and the Soviet invasion combined to force a Japanese surrender, it is unlikely that either one alone would have ended the war as quickly. The use of the bomb was a stunning and demoralizing blow for the Japanese government and population, but it did not cause the emperor or his chief advisers to decide immediately to accept the Potsdam Proclamation. Some scholars have argued that the Soviet strike in Manchuria would have been enough to cause a surrender, and it appears that American military leaders, who thought Soviet entry would be helpful but not decisive, underestimated the potential impact of the Soviet attack on the Japanese leadership. But if the bomb had not been dropped, the end of the war would not have occurred as soon. For one thing, the use of the bomb motivated Stalin to begin the assault on Manchuria several days earlier than planned. More importantly, it is far from clear that the Japanese would have surrendered at once in response to the invasion of Manchuria alone. Suzuki commented after first learning of the offensive, "If we meet the Soviet advance as we are now, we will not be able to hold on for two months." This was an ambiguous statement that nevertheless suggested that Japan would fight on as long as it was able. In short, it required both the atomic bomb and Soviet entry to convince Japanese authorities in Tokyo to accept the Potsdam Proclamation and to force a prompt surrender.[23]

The Soviet attack had another important and often overlooked benefit. It was apparently vital in winning acceptance of the Japanese decision to surrender among military leaders of intact Japanese forces in China and other parts of Asia and the Pacific. This could not be taken for granted. High-level officials in both Washington and Tokyo worried that mutinous generals of Japanese armies abroad would refuse to heed the emperor's wishes. There were millions of able-bodied soldiers stationed in territories the Japanese had conquered early in the war who had been bypassed in the American island campaigns. They had the capacity to continue to battle fiercely and fanatically, and there were disturbing indications that some military leaders might order them to keep fighting. The commander of the Japanese army in China, for example, declared: "Such a disgrace as the surrender of several million troops without fighting is not paralleled in the world's military history, and it is absolutely impossible to submit to unconditional surrender." The invasion of Manchuria quickly neutralized this threat because of the power of the Soviet war machine, and a potentially severe crisis was averted. "Ending the war in the organized capitulation of Japan and her armed forces," historian Richard B. Frank has written, "was a near miraculous deliverance."[24]

The effect of the atomic bomb dropped on Nagasaki is more difficult to assess than the impact of the Hiroshima attack and the Soviet invasion. The second atomic strike discredited the arguments of the die-hard military faction that the United States had only one atomic bomb. At the same time, both bombs made it easier for those who had called for a final battle in the homeland to go along with the emperor's desire for peace, because the new technology diverted blame for the nation's defeat from its military leaders. Nevertheless, the impact of the Nagasaki bomb on Japanese decision-makers was slight in comparison with Hiroshima and the Soviet offensive.

It is possible, perhaps likely, that the war would have ended as soon even if the atomic bomb had not been used against Nagasaki. But the order to drop the second bomb "as soon as made ready" had gone out on July 25, and American leaders had no reason to change it. If the Japanese government had been ready to surrender at the time of the bombing of Hiroshima, as some critics of Truman later charged, it had ample time to notify the United States before the attack on Nagasaki. But Japanese leaders did not act quickly, resolutely, or prudently to end the war even in the face of disaster. They forfeited the opportunity to halt the "rain of ruin" from both atomic and conventional bombs by failing to immediately seek peace.

Even without the use of the atomic bombs, the war would probably have ended before an American invasion of Kyushu became necessary. Conditions in Japan were steadily deteriorating before the atomic attacks and would have continued to worsen as the war dragged on. The distribution of food in Japan was heavily dependent on railroad transportation by the summer of 1945, and as the war drew to an end the United States was planning a major bombing campaign to destroy the rail system. Had the war continued, the Japanese population faced the grim prospect of mass starvation. Diminishing food supplies, the destruction of cities from B-29 raids, and decreasing public morale had already fostered enough discontent to worry the emperor and his advisers. The peace advocates concluded that surrendering with assurances about the status of the emperor was the best way, perhaps the only way, to preserve the national polity. Even without the atomic attacks, it seems likely that the emperor at some point would have acted in the same way that he did in the aftermath of Hiroshima to end the war. Once the emperor decided in favor of surrender, the die-hard militants would probably have gone along, however grudgingly, just as they did when Hirohito supported the peace faction after Hiroshima.

It appears probable that the emperor would have moved to end the war before an American invasion. The fact that the invasion was a dreadful prospect for American leaders and soldiers should not obscure the fact that the costs in lives and destruction would have been even greater for the Japanese. In light of the hardships that Japan was suffering, growing popular criticism of the government, and the intervention of the emperor once he clearly opted for peace, it seems reasonable to conclude that a combination of the B-29 raids with conventional bombs, the blockade, the Soviet invasion, and perhaps a moderation of the unconditional surrender policy would have ended the war without an invasion and without the use of atomic bombs. Although the militants were impervious to the suffering of civilians and welcomed the prospect of an invasion, Kido and presumably Hirohito were much more concerned about a loss of popular support that could threaten the national polity.[25]

After the war was over, a number of high-ranking American leaders, in memoirs or other statements, suggested that even without the use of atomic bombs, an invasion would not have been necessary to secure victory. Among those who made this point were Admiral Leahy, General LeMay, General Arnold, Admiral King, General Eaker, and General Eisenhower.[26] Herbert Feis, a former State Department official and a Pulitzer Prize–winning historian, reported in a book published in 1966 that Secretary of the Navy Forrestal, Undersecretary of the Navy Bard, and General Spaatz shared the same opinion.[27] Of course, this conclusion was an after-the-fact appraisal on the part of former policymakers and military authorities. With the exception of LeMay, there is no evidence that the postwar statements of American leaders reflected their judgment during the summer of 1945 or that any of them, with the possible exception of Bard, informed Truman that they thought the war could end without the bomb or an invasion. Important information about Japan's weakness and growing popular discontent among the Japanese did not surface until after the war and was not available to Truman before Hiroshima.

Some of the officials who asserted after the fact that the war could have ended on a satisfactory basis without the bomb or an invasion were influenced by bureaucratic interests, personal experiences, or even political ambitions. Navy leaders were concerned that the importance of their mission would not receive due recognition in the postwar world and that their status, prestige, and budgets would suffer accordingly. Air force leaders wanted the establishment of a separate branch of the armed forces that was independent of the Army. In both cases, they did not want the effects of the atomic bombs to overshadow their contributions to the victory over Japan. Leahy belonged to the old-fashioned school of military ethics that deplored attacks on civilian populations. He found the atomic bomb barbaric, which affected the conclusion in his memoirs that the use of atomic bombs "was of no material assistance in our war against Japan."[28] Eisenhower, when he published his wartime memoirs in 1948, might have wanted to present an image of a military leader who was tough but sensitive to the horrors of war.[29]

Despite personal backgrounds or experiences that might have colored their views, the independent testimonies of so many top officials about the likelihood of the war ending without an invasion or the bomb should not be lightly dismissed. They almost certainly would have refrained from promoting an argument that could offend the president they had served or invite criticism unless their assessment had some solid factual or analytical foundations. Most of them had retired from active service by the time they published their memoirs, so they were removed from interservice rivalries and bureaucratic posturing. Their judgments were not conclusive, but they provided substantial confirmatory evidence that victory over Japan could have been achieved without either the bomb or an invasion.

Although information and testimonies that appeared after the war suggested that neither the bomb nor the invasion was essential to force a Japanese surrender, documentary sources do not demonstrate that high U.S. officials were convinced in the summer of 1945 that victory would be accomplished without a landing on Kyushu. They could not be certain that the war would end before November 1, and they proceeded on the assumption that the invasion would be necessary. American leaders and military planners regarded an invasion as a genuine possibility for which preparations had to be made. But they did not view it as inevitable; it was a contingency if all else failed to end the war. Deputy Chief of Staff Thomas Handy told Stimson on June 4 that it would take Soviet entry into the war and a landing "or imminent threat of a landing" to bring about the surrender.[30] General Marshall used a similar conditional reference at the June 18 meeting at which Truman authorized the Kyushu invasion. He commented that Soviet participation in the war would help force a surrender "if we land in Japan."[31] A member of Marshall's staff, General George A. Lincoln, wrote to a colleague on July 10, 1945: "The B-29s are doing such a swell job that some people think the Japs will quit without an invasion."[32] One of MacArthur's lieutenants, General Robert Eichelberger, told his wife on July 24 that "a great many people, probably 50%, feel that Japan is about to fold up."[33]

Truman's diary notations support the same conclusion. His remark after meeting with Stalin on July 17, "Fini Japs when that [Soviet entry into the war] comes about," does not prove that he thought the Soviet invasion of Manchuria was enough in itself to force an early surrender. It does, however, suggest that he did not believe an invasion was inevitable. This also applies to Truman's notation the following day: "Believe Japs will fold up before Russia comes in. I am sure they will when Manhattan appears over their homeland." The precise meaning of those comments in perhaps debatable, but they clearly suggest the president thought that even if the bomb was not used, the war might end without an invasion.

A further indication of the same outcome was the reconsideration in early August 1945 of the plans for the American landing on Kyushu. Intelligence information showed that Japanese forces in southern Kyushu were much larger than anticipated, and this caused military planners to weigh the possibility of shifting the site of the invasion or perhaps even canceling it. The end of the war made this problem moot, but it is further evidence that Truman did not face a clearly defined choice between the atomic bomb and an invasion of Japan.[34]

Given the fact that Truman and his top-level advisers did not regard an invasion as inevitable and given their knowledge, incomplete as it was, of the severity of the crisis in Japan, the question arises of why they did not elect to wait to use the bomb. The invasion was not scheduled until November 1, 1945, so why not postpone the atomic attacks and hope that Japan collapsed under the weight of the critical internal and external problems it faced? Why rush to drop the atomic bombs when they might prove to be unnecessary? Five fundamental considerations, all of which grew out of circumstances that existed in the summer of 1945, moved Truman to use the bombs immediately, without a great deal of thought and without consulting with his advisers about the advantages and potential disadvantages of the new weapons: (1) the commitment to ending the war successfully at the earliest possible moment; (2) the need to justify the effort and expense of building the atomic bombs; (3) the hope of achieving diplomatic gains in the growing rivalry with the Soviet Union; (4) the lack of incentives not to use atomic weapons; and (5) hatred of the Japanese and a desire for vengeance.

Ending the war at the earliest possible moment. Truman was looking for a way to end the war as quickly and painlessly as possible for the United States; he was not looking for a way to avoid using the bomb. The primary objective of the United States had always been to win the war decisively at the lowest cost in American casualties, and the bomb was the best means to accomplish those goals. Even if the bomb was not necessary to end the war without an invasion, it was necessary to end the war as soon as possible. Although American forces were not involved in any major campaigns at the time of the Japanese surrender, they were still suffering casualties. If the total of 3,233 Army combat and noncombat deaths in the month of July 1945 is taken as a norm—a risky assumption, but they are the only relevant figures available—the continuation of the war for, say, another three months until the invasion was scheduled to begin would have resulted in approximately 9,700 American deaths in the Army alone. If only combat deaths are considered, the 775 sustained in July would extrapolate into about 2,300 had the war lasted three months more. The overall number of American casualties would have increased further from Japanese attacks on U.S. ships; the battle of Okinawa and the sinking of the *Indianapolis* demonstrated how high the costs to the Navy could be.

If Truman had been confronted with a choice, on the one hand, of using the atomic bomb or, on the other hand, permitting the deaths of 9,700 soldiers and a significant number of sailors, there is no reason to believe that he would have refrained from authorizing the bomb. He would almost certainly have made the same choice if the number of projected American casualties had been much smaller. Whatever casualty estimates he might have received or projected, he was strongly committed to reducing them to a minimum. This goal was consistent with American war aims and with his own experience. The atomic bomb offered the way most likely to achieve an American victory on American terms with the lowest cost in American lives.

The inflated numbers of American lives supposedly saved by the bomb, numbers cited by Truman and others after the war, should not obscure the fact that the president would have elected to use the bomb even if the numbers of U.S. casualties prevented had been relatively small.[35] In two statements he made on August 9, the president suggested that the bomb would spare thousands, but not hundreds of thousands, of American lives. In a radio address to the nation he declared that he had used the bomb "to shorten the agony of war, in order to save the lives of thousands and thousands of young Americans." In a congratulatory message to the men and women of the Manhattan Project, he expressed hope that "this new weapon will result in the saving of thousands of American lives."[36] By citing the number of Americans who would be spared in a range of thousands, Truman's statements were more in line with the military's estimates in the summer of 1945 than with later claims that the bomb saved hundreds of thousands of lives.

Even though American policymakers did not regard an invasion as inevitable, they did regard it as possible. They could not be sure that the Japanese would surrender without an invasion. With information that became available later, it is possible to determine with greater certainty that victory would have come without a landing on Kyushu. This is, however, an after-the-fact conclusion that cannot be proven, and it is essential to keep in mind that Truman and his advisers had to make their decisions based on what they knew at the time.

Justifying the costs of the Manhattan Project. As a corollary, and only as a corollary, to the main objective of shortening the war and saving American lives, Truman wanted to justify the expense and effort required to build the atomic bombs. After learning of Hiroshima, Byrnes commented that he had been "worried about the huge expendtirue [*sic*] and feared repercussions because he had doubt of its working." Throughout the war Groves and his superiors in the War Department also fretted about the possibility that after spending huge amounts of money and procuring vital war supplies on a priority basis, the bomb would be a dud. They could easily imagine being grilled mercilessly by hostile members of Congress. The success of the Manhattan Project in building the bombs and ending the war was a source of satisfaction and relief.[37]

Truman's concerns were broader. If he had not used the bomb once it became available, he could never have explained his reasoning in a way that satisfied the American people, particularly those who lost loved ones in the last few days or weeks of the war. As Stimson wrote in 1947: "My chief purpose was to end the war in victory with the least possible cost in the lives of the men in the armies which I had helped to raise. . . . I believe that no man, in our position and subject to our responsibilities, holding in his hands a weapon of such possibilities for accomplishing this purpose and saving those lives, could have failed to use it and afterwards looked his countrymen in the face."[38] If Truman had backed off from using a weapon that had cost the United States dearly to build, with the result that more American troops died, public confidence in his capacity to govern would have been, at best, severely undermined.

Impressing the Soviets. As an added incentive, using the bomb might provide diplomatic benefits by making the Soviet Union more amenable to American wishes. There is no question that Byrnes strongly believed the bomb would improve his negotiating position with the Soviets over the growing list of contested issues. Byrnes enjoyed easy access to and great influence with Truman on diplomatic issues; the president acquiesced in Byrnes's efforts to delay Soviet entry into the Pacific war and, from all indications, shared his hope that the bomb would provide diplomatic benefits by making the Soviets more tractable. But Truman did not drop the bomb primarily to intimidate or impress the Soviets. If its use resulted in diplomatic advantages, that would be, as Barton J. Bernstein has argued, a "bonus."[39]

Truman's foremost consideration in using the bomb immediately was not to frustrate Soviet ambitions in Asia or to show off the bomb before the Japanese capitulated; it was to end the war at the earliest possible time. Despite their impatience with Soviet demands at Potsdam, he and Byrnes still hoped that they could get along with Stalin in the postwar era. Growing differences with the Soviet Union were a factor in the thinking of American officials about the bomb but were not the main reason they rushed to drop it on Japan.

Lack of incentives not to use the bomb. Truman used the bomb because he had no compelling reason to avoid using it. American leaders had always assumed that the bomb would be dropped when it became available, and there were no military, diplomatic, political, or moral considerations that undermined or reversed that assumption. Indeed, military, diplomatic, and political considerations weighed heavily in favor of the use of the bomb. Militarily, it could speed the end of the war. Diplomatically, it could make the Soviets more likely to accept American positions. Politically, ending the war quickly would be enormously popular, while delaying the achievement of victory by not using the bomb could be disastrous.

Moral scruples about using the bomb were not a major deterrent to its use. American policymakers took the same view that General LeMay advanced later in his memoirs: "From a practical standpoint of the soldiers out in the field it doesn't make any difference how you slay an enemy. Everybody worries about their own losses."[40] Bombing of civilians was such an established practice by the summer of 1945 that American leaders accepted it as a legitimate means of conducting war. It seemed defensible if it shortened the war and saved American lives, and that was the principal purpose of dropping the atomic bomb. Some high-ranking American officials found attacks on civilian targets distasteful, and Truman, after he saw the photographs of and read the reports about the destruction of Hiroshima, was so disturbed that he issued an order that no more atomic bombs be used without his express authorization. But moral reservations about terror bombing remained muted; on balance they were less influential than the desire to end the war as soon as possible. In the minds of American policymakers, this objective took precedence over moral considerations about the indiscriminate bombing of civilian populations.

Dealing with "a beast." Hatred of the Japanese, a desire for revenge for Pearl Harbor, and racist attitudes were a part of the mix of motives that led to the atomic attacks. When Samuel McCrea Cavert, general secretary of the Federal Council of Churches, raised objections to the atomic bombings, Truman responded on August 11, 1945: "Nobody is more disturbed over the use of Atomic bombs than I am but I was greatly disturbed over the unwarranted attack by the Japanese on Pearl Harbor and their murder of our prisoners of war.... When you have to deal with a beast you have to treat him as a beast. It is most regrettable but nevertheless true."[41] Truman did not authorize the bombs solely or primarily for those reasons, and there is no reason to think that he would have refrained from using atomic weapons against Germany if they had been available before the European war ended. But the prevalent loathing of Japan, among policymakers and the American people alike, helped override any hesitation or ambivalence that Truman and his advisers might have felt about the use of atomic bombs.

All of those considerations played a role in the thinking of American leaders, and taken together they made the use of the bomb an easy and obvious decision. It was not an action they relished, but neither was it one they agonized over. The use of the bomb was not inevitable; if Truman had been seeking a way to avoid dropping it, he could have done so. But in the context of the circumstances in the summer of 1945 and in light of the disadvantages of the alternatives, it is difficult to imagine Truman or any other American president electing not to use the bomb.

The fundamental question that has triggered debate about Truman's decision since shortly after the end of World War II is, Was the bomb necessary? In view of the evidence now available, the answer is yes ... and no. Yes, the bomb was necessary, in combination with the Soviet attack on Manchuria, to end the war at the earliest possible moment. And yes, the bomb was necessary to save the lives of American troops, perhaps numbering in the several thousands. But no, the bomb was probably not necessary to end the war within a fairly short time without an invasion of Japan. And no, the bomb was not necessary to save the lives of *hundreds* of thousands of American troops.

7

Hiroshima in History

In the immediate aftermath of the war, the use of atomic bombs received the overwhelming approval of the American people. A Gallup poll conducted on August 26, 1945, for example, showed that 85 percent of the respondents endorsed the atomic attacks, while 10 percent opposed and 5 percent had no opinion. Another survey taken in the fall of 1945 produced similar findings. Only 4.5 percent of those questioned believed that the United States should not have used atomic weapons, while 53.5 percent expressed unequivocal support for the bombings of Hiroshima and Nagasaki. Another 22.7 percent wished that the United States had dropped "many more" atomic bombs on Japan before its surrender.[1]

There were, however, a few critics who questioned the need for and the morality of dropping the atomic bombs. Pacifist groups, a number of atomic scientists, some religious leaders and organizations, and a scattering of political commentators, both liberal and conservative, condemned the atomic attacks because of their indiscriminate killing of civilians and/or the failure of the United States to give Japan an explicit warning about the bomb before Hiroshima. As time went on, other voices raised new misgivings about the use of the atomic bombs. Norman Cousins, editor of the *Saturday Review of Literature*, and Thomas K. Finletter, a former assistant secretary of state, suggested in June 1946 that Truman's use of the bomb might have been prompted more by a desire for diplomatic gains in the growing rivalry with the Soviet Union than by military necessity. Writer John Hersey, although he did not express an opinion on the bombings, put human faces on six of the survivors and the trials they endured in a widely publicized article in the *New Yorker* in August 1946.[2]

The final report of the United States Strategic Bombing Survey, published in July 1946, implicitly questioned the official rationale that the atomic bombings had been necessary to force a Japanese surrender and avoid an invasion. At the request of President Truman, the survey conducted a study of the effects of American aerial attacks on Japan as well as an analysis of Japan's "struggle to end the war."

After examining documents and interviewing Japanese officials, it concluded that Japan would have surrendered without the use of atomic bombs, Soviet entry into the war, or an American invasion of Kyushu. "Based on a detailed investigation of all the facts, and supported by the testimony of the surviving Japanese leaders involved," the report declared, "it is the Survey's opinion that certainly prior to 31 December 1945, and in all probability prior to 1 November 1945, Japan would have surrendered even if the atomic bombs had not been dropped, even if Russia had not entered the war, and even if no invasion had been planned or contemplated."[3]

The survey's statement was less conclusive than it appeared. It was a "counterfactual" argument, meaning that it was based not on hard evidence but on speculation about what might have happened. The counterfactual judgment was largely the product of Paul Nitze, the vice chairman of the survey team, who believed that the bomb had not been essential for forcing a surrender. The interviews of Japanese officials did not uniformly or even largely support the idea that the war would have ended without the bomb, the Soviet declaration of war on Japan, or an American invasion. Indeed, many suggested that the bomb was the key to bringing about the surrender. As always in dealing with counterfactuals, there is no way of proving or disproving the survey's conclusion, and it cannot be viewed as definitive.[4]

The criticisms of the atomic attacks and the conclusions of the Strategic Bombing Survey had very little discernible impact on popular support for Truman's decision. Although the existence of atomic weapons and the possibility that they might at some time be used against American cities was troubling, they did not lead to widespread reappraisal or disapproval of the use of atomic bombs against Japan. Nevertheless, even occasional expressions of dissent offended some Manhattan Project veterans. One leading figure in the building of the bomb, James B. Conant, decided to take action to counter the critics. Conant, a prominent chemist and president of Harvard University, had played a major role in the development of the bomb as the deputy director of the Office of Scientific Research and Development and head of the National Defense Research Committee, both of which had mobilized scientific research in support of the war effort.

Conant, like other atomic scientists, had not been a part of Truman's inner circle that made decisions regarding the use of the bomb. He had, however, occupied a position in which he offered scientific expertise and policy judgments to Groves, Stimson, and other top officials. As a member of the Interim Committee, he had suggested in a meeting of May 31, 1945, "that the most desirable target [for an atomic bomb] would be a vital war plant . . . closely surrounded by workers' houses."[5] Conant fully supported the use of atomic bombs against Japan, in part because he shared with American policymakers the objective of achieving a decisive victory as quickly as possible. In addition, Conant, along with a number of other Manhattan Project scientists, favored the use of the bomb as a means to promote postwar peace. This objective was not an important consideration for Truman and his close advisers, but it was a key element in the thinking of Conant and other scientists.

Conant was convinced that a combat demonstration of the destructive power of atomic bombs was essential to prevent their future use. It was, he believed, "the only way to awaken the world to the necessity of abolishing war altogether."[6] Along with scientific advisers to the Interim Committee and other colleagues, Conant reasoned that the use of the bomb would not only force a prompt Japanese surrender but also shock leaders around the globe into seeking international control of nuclear weapons. "We have had some skeptics express doubts as to whether [the bomb] is indeed a revolutionary weapon," he remarked in 1947, "but what skepticism there would have been had there been no actual use in war!"[7]

Conant had little patience with critics of the use of the bomb against Japan. Although their influence was slight, he worried about the consequences if they undermined public support for Truman's decision. One harmful result might be that the chances for arms control would be diminished. Conant believed that only if the American people clearly demonstrated their willingness to use their atomic arsenal would the Soviet Union be amenable to nuclear arms control agreements. Further, he feared that questions about the use of the bomb would influence teachers and students in the future in ways that distorted history. "You may be inclined to dismiss all this talk [criticizing the use of the bomb] as representing only a small minority of the population, which I think it does," Conant told a friend in September 1946. "However, this type of sentimentalism, for so I regard it, is bound to have a great deal of influence on the next generation. The type of person who goes in to teaching, particularly school teaching, will be influenced a great deal by this type of argument."[8]

In order to head off the potential influence of those who raised doubts about whether the dropping of atomic bombs on Japan had been a sound and proper action, Conant persuaded Henry L. Stimson to write an article to explain why they were used. Stimson, who was writing his memoirs in retirement, reluctantly took on the assignment, assisted by the collaborator on his memoirs, McGeorge Bundy, the son of former War Department aide Harvey H. Bundy and future national security adviser to presidents John F. Kennedy and Lyndon B. Johnson. The article, which appeared in the February 1947 issue of *Harper's Magazine*, deliberately refrained from directly challenging the critics of the use of the bomb. It provided a judicious, dispassionate, and seemingly authoritative treatment of the Manhattan Project and the decision to drop the bomb, complete with excerpts from Stimson's diary and other documents. It presented the use of the bomb as the "least abhorrent choice" that accomplished its objective of ending the war quickly. Stimson reported that the atomic attacks were authorized in order to avoid an invasion of Japan, which, he said, might have been "expected to cost over a million casualties to American forces alone."[9]

More than any other single publication, Stimson's article influenced popular views about Truman's decision to use the bomb. The information it provided and the respect its author commanded made its arguments seem unassailable. The article received wide circulation and acclaim, and Conant was satisfied that it had fulfilled his objective of effectively countering the complaints of those who criticized the use of the bomb. However, the article, despite the aura of authority it presented, was not a full accounting; it glossed over or omitted important aspects of the events that led to the bombing of Hiroshima and Nagasaki. It offered only hints of alternatives to the use of the bomb or Stimson's own support for modifying the demand for unconditional surrender. It failed to cite the influence of diplomatic considerations and gave the misleading impression that Truman and his advisers carefully considered whether or not the bomb should be dropped. The most vivid of the article's arguments was that the use of the bomb prevented over 1 million American casualties by making an invasion unnecessary. The source of Stimson's figure is not clear; even Bundy could not recall precisely the basis for the casualty estimate.[10] Stimson was not the first to suggest the figure of 1 million, but after his article appeared, that number, or often an embellished variation of it, became indelibly etched into the mythology of the decision to use the bomb.

On at least one occasion, Truman drew on Stimson's casualty estimate in his own explanation for the use of the bomb. In December 1952, James L. Cate, an editor and author of the U.S. Air Force's history of World War II, wrote to Truman for information on some issues relating to the bomb. Truman drafted a handwritten reply in which he claimed that during a meeting with advisers at Potsdam in which the use of the bomb was considered, Marshall told him that an invasion would cost a minimum of 250,000 casualties. When a member of the White House staff saw Truman's response to Cate, he recommended that the casualty estimate be raised to conform with the projection of 1 million that Stimson had used in his *Harper's* article. Truman accepted the change and cited the larger number in his reply to Cate. The letter's accuracy was doubtful not only because of the revised casualty figure but also because the meeting at Potsdam that the president mentioned almost certainly never took place. There is no evidence that supports Truman's recollection of the conference he described. But the letter to Cate contributed to the unfounded impression that Truman and his advisers had carefully weighed the decision to drop the bomb and that their action had saved American forces from suffering hundreds of thousands of casualties.[11]

Truman used different numbers at different times when he discussed the estimated losses that the bomb had prevented, and he sometimes obscured the distinction between casualties and fatalities. In his memoirs, published in 1955, he stated that Marshall informed him "it might cost half a million American lives to force the enemy's surrender on his home grounds." In other cases he claimed that the use of the bomb saved 250,000 American lives (1946), a quarter of a million American lives and "an equal number of Japanese young men" (1948), one-half million casualties (1949), "millions of lives" (1959), and the lives of 125,000 Americans and 125,000 "Japanese youngsters" (1963). The casualty estimates that Truman cited were obviously not a fixed number, perhaps because he had never been informed of such high figures before he authorized the dropping of the bomb.[12]

Truman's claims were supported by other leading military and political figures, including Churchill, Marshall, Groves, and Byrnes, who also contended in postwar statements or memoirs that the bomb saved hundreds of thousands of American lives.[13] This explanation for the use of the bomb, advanced by respected high-level officials, came to be accepted as a statement of unqualified fact by most Americans. With few documents open for scholarly research, there was little basis for questioning the claims of policymakers on why they opted for the bomb. As a result, the myth took hold—Truman faced a stark choice between using the bomb or sacrificing the lives of huge numbers of American soldiers.

The first scholarly history of the decision to use the bomb raised some questions about the standard view without undermining its basic premises. In *Japan Subdued: The Atomic Bomb and the End of the War in the Pacific*, published in 1961, former State Department official Herbert Feis concluded that "the impelling reason for the decision to use [the bomb] was military—to end the war victoriously as soon as possible." He accepted the argument that if an invasion had been necessary, it might have cost hundreds of thousands of America lives. But Feis discussed alternatives to the bomb at length, expressed regret that the United States did not give Japan an explicit warning about the pending use of atomic weapons at the time of the Potsdam Proclamation, and agreed with the conclusion of the Strategic Bombing Survey that the war would have ended by the end of 1945 without the bomb, Soviet entry into the war, or an American invasion. And although he supported the claims of hundreds of thousands of American casualties or deaths in an invasion, he admitted that he could not find evidence to confirm those estimates.[14]

In 1965, political economist Gar Alperovitz published a book titled *Atomic Diplomacy*, which was based on his doctoral dissertation. He challenged the traditional explanation more directly and much more critically than Feis had done by suggesting that the bomb had not been needed to end the war at the earliest possible time. Drawing on recently opened sources, especially the papers and diary of Henry L. Stimson, he asserted that the United States dropped it more for political than for military reasons. Alperovitz argued that Truman did not seriously consider alternatives to the bomb because he wanted to impress the Soviets with its power. In his analysis, the bomb was used primarily to intimidate the Soviets rather than to defeat the Japanese. Alperovitz pointed out that many sources were still not available to scholars and clearly stated that his findings could not be regarded as conclusive.[15]

Atomic Diplomacy received a great deal of popular and scholarly attention and triggered a spirited historiographical debate. By the mid-1970s, after the publication of several works that drew on extensive research in primary sources, including important studies by Barton J. Bernstein and Martin J. Sherwin, scholars reached a general consensus that combined the traditional interpretation with Alperovitz's "revisionist" position. They concluded that the primary motivation for dropping the bomb was to end the war with Japan but that diplomatic considerations played a significant, if secondary, role in the Truman administration's view of the new weapon's value.[16]

Over the next 15 years, new evidence relating to the use of the bomb stirred further scholarly investigation and debate. It included a handwritten diary that Truman jotted down at Potsdam and personal letters that he sent to Mrs. Truman. Those documents greatly enriched the record on the president's views of the bomb in the summer of 1945, but they did not provide conclusive evidence on his thoughts about the likelihood that the war would end without an invasion, the need for the bomb, the role of diplomatic considerations in deciding to use the bomb, or the extent to which he weighed those issues. In a similar manner, the opening of personal papers and official records of other high-level policymakers and their staffs in the 1970s and 1980s broadened the documentary base for studying the decision to use the bomb but did not offer definitive answers to questions that had intrigued scholars and sometimes provoked sharp debate among them.

Nevertheless, by the late 1980s, specialists who studied the available evidence reached a broad, though hardly unanimous, consensus on some key issues surrounding the use of the bomb. One point of agreement was that Truman and his advisers were well aware of alternatives to the bomb that seemed likely, but not certain, to end the war within a relatively short time. Another was that an invasion of Japan would probably not have been necessary to achieve victory. A third point of general agreement in the scholarly literature on the decision to use the bomb was that the postwar claims that the bomb prevented hundreds of thousands of American combat deaths could not be sustained with the available evidence. Most students of the subject also concurred that political considerations figured in the deliberations about the implications of the bomb and the end of the war with Japan. On all of those points, the scholarly consensus rejected the traditional view that the bomb was the only alternative to an invasion of Japan that would have cost a huge number of American lives. At the same time, most scholars supported the claim of Truman and his advisers that the primary motivation for dropping atomic bombs on Hiroshima and Nagasaki was to end the war at the earliest possible moment—that is, for military reasons.[17]

The debates among scholars and the conclusions that they reached about the decision to use the bomb were not widely known to the general public, which from all indications remained wedded to the traditional view that Truman faced a categorical choice between the bomb and an enormously costly invasion. The chasm between the myth that the public embraced and the findings of scholars who examined the documentary evidence led to a bitter controversy when the Smithsonian Institution's National Air and Space Museum made plans in the early 1990s to present a major exhibit on the bomb and the end of World War II. The show would be built around a section of the restored fuselage of the *Enola Gay*, the plane that dropped the atomic bomb on Hiroshima (the entire plane was too large to display). Museum curators designed an exhibit that was intended both to commemorate the valor and sacrifices of American war veterans and to reflect scholarly findings on the decision to use the bomb. But this proved to be an impossible task. By raising questions about the traditional and popularly accepted interpretation of why the United States dropped the bomb, the original script for the exhibit set off a firestorm of protest.

Critics of the script complained that the planned *Enola Gay* exhibit was unduly disparaging of American actions and unduly sympathetic toward the Japanese. Representatives of the Air Force Association, an organization established after World War II to promote air power that included many veterans among its membership, took the lead in denouncing the script. By distorting or quoting out of context some of the statements in the draft script, the association made the proposed show seem outrageously one-sided. It soon won allies from other veterans' groups, many members of Congress, and most newspapers. The *Wall Street Journal* spoke for many critics of the planned exhibit in August 1994 when it condemned "scriptwriters [who] disdain any belief that the decision to drop the bomb could have been inspired by something other than racism or bloodlust."[18]

The original script had hardly been flawless. Robert C. Post, a curator at the Smithsonian at the time and a keen chronicler of the museum's history, later wrote that it was "needlessly, even recklessly, inflammatory." The Smithsonian responded to the protests by modifying the script, especially by correcting parts that demonstrated a lack of balance. Among other changes, it placed greater emphasis on Japanese atrocities during the war and less emphasis on the victims of the atomic attacks. But it became apparent that the most adamant critics would not find acceptable any script that raised questions about the mythological explanation for the use of the bomb. Historians who defended the script pointed out that a vast volume of historical evidence did not confirm the view that Truman faced a stark choice between the bomb and an invasion, but their arguments made no discernible impact on those who objected to the exhibit.

In early 1995, the Smithsonian bowed to enormous and irresistible political pressure and drastically scaled back the planned exhibit. It decided to display a section of the *Enola Gay* with a minimum of commentary. The head of the Smithsonian, secretary I. Michael Heyman, announced that the exhibit would just "report the facts." The "facts" that the exhibit reported when it opened in June 1995 were largely innocuous descriptions of the plane and its restoration. But some statements were disputable assertions about the use of the bomb, assertions that were highly interpretive. One label, for example, declared that the use of atomic bombs "made unnecessary the planned invasion of the Japanese home islands" and that "such an invasion would have led to very heavy casualties among American, Allied, and Japanese armed forces, and Japanese civilians." Those statements were not necessarily inaccurate; after all, at the time of Hiroshima the United States was making plans for an invasion in case it proved to be necessary, and "very heavy" U.S. casualties could have referred to the estimates of military planners in the summer of 1945. But the effect of this label on most who read it was probably to reinforce their existing impression that Truman faced a choice between dropping the bomb and ordering an invasion. In the *Enola Gay* exhibit, the myths about the decision to use the bomb prevailed over historical evidence that revealed the complexities of the events and considerations that led to Hiroshima and Nagasaki.[19]

The *Enola Gay* controversy highlighted the gap between scholarly and popular views on the use of the bomb. Over a period of 20 years after the angry recriminations that erupted over the Smithsonian's plans, scholars continued to mine a rich abundance of documentary sources on the subject. Most of them rejected the two polar interpretations of Truman's decision. The flaws of the traditional view that Truman's only reasonable alternative to an invasion was the bomb had long been evident, at least since Herbert Feis had published his book in 1961. The revisionist view that the bomb was unnecessary because Japan was on the verge of surrender has been conclusively undermined by the opening of valuable Japanese materials after Hirohito's death in 1989. "The myth that the Japanese were ready to surrender," historian Max Hastings wrote in 2007, "has been so comprehensively discredited by modern research that it is astonishing some writers continue to give it credence." Most scholars took a balanced, middle-ground position that combined elements of the competing arguments and did not offer support to purists at either pole of the interpretive spectrum.[20]

Despite the broad agreement among specialists on important aspects of the topic, many of the key issues that divide scholars on the decision to use the bomb cannot be resolved because they are counterfactual. The lack of conclusive evidence that could settle points of dispute is, of course, a problem that faces historians in the study of any subject. But the debate over the decision to use the atomic bomb hinges more than most topics on "might-have-beens" and "never-weres." Those issues involve questions that can be evaluated only with incomplete factual evidence or debatable analysis. The presence of counterfactual issues in the controversies over Hiroshima is not new; the traditional interpretation relied heavily on unprovable assertions about the need for an invasion and the number of casualties it would have caused.

The most important issues that cannot be fully settled because they require speculation and extrapolation from available evidence include (1) how long the war would have continued if the bomb had not been used; (2) how many casualties American forces would have suffered if the bomb had not been dropped; (3) whether an invasion would have been necessary without the use of the bomb; (4) the number of American lives and casualties an invasion would have exacted had it proven necessary; (5) whether Japan would have responded favorably to an American offer to allow the emperor to remain on the throne before Hiroshima, or whether such an offer would have prolonged the war; and (6) whether any of the other alternatives to the use of the bomb would have ended the war as quickly on a basis satisfactory to the United States.

Those questions go to the heart of historiographical disputes among scholars on Truman's decision to use the atomic bomb. They cannot be answered in a way that will be accepted by all scholars or more casual students interested in the topic. The traditional view of the use of the bomb that Stimson and Truman and many others advanced after World War II was appealing in part because it was unambiguous. If Truman had in fact faced a choice between authorizing the bomb and ordering an invasion that would have cost hundreds of thousands of American lives, the decision to use the bomb would have been obvious and, in the minds of most Americans then and later, incontestable. But the existence of evidence that shows a vastly more complex situation introduces ambiguity and controversy into the issue. The best that scholars can do in addressing the issues is to draw conclusions based on sources that help reconstruct the context of events in the summer of 1945.

The question of the morality of Truman's decision, which is often an unstated part of the debate among historians, will likewise remain unresolved. Scholars who have offered moral judgments on Truman's action range widely in their assessments, from arguments that it was entirely justified by Japanese aggression and refusal to surrender to suggestions that the use of the bomb was the moral equivalent of the Nazi

Holocaust. No amount of historical evidence will bridge this gap; it arises to a large degree from the differing values, assumptions, priorities, and experiences that individual scholars bring to their work on the subject. The information that historians provide will not settle the moral issues. As historian Charles S. Maier has suggested in a somewhat different context: "Maybe God draws bottom lines; historians need only record the entries in the ledger."[21]

Recording the entries in the ledger accurately requires recognizing the complexities and uncertainties of the issues surrounding the use of the bomb. Within that context, the answer to the fundamental question that has stirred so much debate among scholars is appropriately ambiguous. The question is, Was the bomb necessary? The answer seems to be yes and no. Yes, it was necessary to end the war as quickly as possible. No, it was not necessary to prevent an invasion of Japan.

A corollary to the first question is, What did the bomb accomplish? The answer seems to be that it shortened the war and saved the lives of a relatively small but far from inconsequential number of Americans. It might also have saved many Japanese lives, though this was not an important consideration for U.S. policymakers. Was that sufficient reason to wipe out two Japanese cities with weapons that delivered unprecedented military power and unpredictable diplomatic consequences? There is no definitive answer to that question or to a multitude of others that follow from it. But it still needs to be addressed in an informed way by scholars, students, and other concerned citizens. The decision to use atomic bombs against Japan was such a momentous event in bringing about the end of World War II and in shaping the postwar world that it should continue to be studied, evaluated, and debated. The issue of whether the destruction of Hiroshima and Nagasaki were sound, proper, and justifiable actions must be approached by fully considering the situation facing American and Japanese leaders in the summer of 1945 and by banishing the myths that have taken hold since then.

CHRONOLOGY

JULY 25   General Handy issues order to use atomic bombs "as soon as made ready."

JULY 26   Potsdam Proclamation published.

JULY 29   USS *Indianapolis* sunk by Japanese submarine.

AUGUST 2   Potsdam Conference ends.

AUGUST 6   Atomic attack on Hiroshima.

AUGUST 7   Japanese government receives authoritative reports about destruction of Hiroshima. Hirohito tells Kido that the war must end quickly.

AUGUST 8   Soviets declare war on Japan.

AUGUST 9   Atomic attack on Nagasaki. Hirohito tells cabinet and the Supreme Council for the Direction of the War that he supports accepting the Potsdam Proclamation if the imperial institution can be retained.

AUGUST 10   Japan transmits message offering to surrender if the imperial institution is allowed to remain.

AUGUST 12   U.S. responds vaguely to Japanese surrender message.

AUGUST 14   Hirohito appeals to the cabinet and Supreme Council for the Direction of the War to accept U.S. surrender terms. They honor his request.

AUGUST 15   Radio broadcast of Hirohito's message to the Japanese people about the end of the war.

SEPTEMBER 2   Surrender documents signed on USS *Missouri*.

NOTES

CHAPTER ONE

1 Robert H. Ferrell, ed., *Off the Record: The Private Papers of Harry S. Truman* (New York: Harper and Row, 1980), 56.

2 Henry L. Stimson and McGeorge Bundy, *On Active Service in Peace and War* (New York: Harper and Brothers, 1947), 637; Henry L. Stimson, "The Decision to Use the Atomic Bomb," *Harper's Magazine* 194 (February 1947): 97–107 (quotation on 102).

3 George F. Kennan, *Memoirs: 1925–1950* (Boston: Little, Brown, 1967), 345.

4 John P. Sutherland, "The Story Gen. Marshall Told Me," *U.S. News and World Report* 47 (November 2, 1959): 50–56 (quotations on 52, 53).

5 Ferrell, *Off the Record*, 49; *New York Times*, August 30, 1945, 1.

6 Harry S. Truman, Speech delivered at Gridiron Dinner, December 15, 1945, Speech File (Longhand Notes), Box 46, President's Secretary's File, Harry S. Truman Papers, Harry S. Truman Library, Independence, Mo.; Truman to James L. Cate, January 12, 1953, in *The Decision to Drop the Atomic Bomb on Japan*, vol. 1 of *Documentary History of the Truman Presidency*, ed. Dennis Merrill (Bethesda, Md.: University Publications of America, 1995), 525–26.

7 "Opinion Outlook," *National Journal* 27 (September 30, 1995): 2444; Pew Research Center, "American, Japanese: Mutual Respect 70 Years After the End of WWII," April 7, 2015, http://www.pewglobal.org/2015/04/07/

americans-japanese-mutual-respect-70-years-after-the-end-of-wwii/#the-role-of-history-in-the-u-s-japan-relationship/ (accessed April 7, 2007).

CHAPTER TWO

1 Alonzo L. Hamby, "An American Democrat: A Reevaluation of the Personality of Harry S. Truman," *Political Science Quarterly* 106 (Spring 1991): 33–55 (quotation on 37). See also Hamby's biography *Man of the People: A Life of Harry S. Truman* (New York: Oxford University Press, 1995).

2 Quoted in David McCullough, *Truman* (New York: Simon and Schuster, 1992), 353.

3 Henry A. Wallace Diary, October 15, 1945, in *The Price of Vision: The Diary of Henry A. Wallace, 1942–1946*, ed. John Morton Blum (Boston: Houghton Mifflin, 1973), 491.

4 *The Public Papers and Addresses of Franklin D. Roosevelt*, comp. Samuel I. Rosenman (New York: Harper and Brothers, 1950), 13: 384.

5 James MacGregor Burns, *Roosevelt: The Soldier of Freedom, 1940–1945* (New York: Harcourt Brace Jovanovich, 1970), 546.

6 Robert H. Ferrell, ed., *Dear Bess: The Letters from Harry to Bess Truman, 1910–1959* (New York: W. W. Norton, 1983), 294.

7 For informed discussions of the roles of Groves and Oppenheimer in the Manhattan Project, see Stanley Goldberg, "Groves and Oppenheimer: The Story of a Partnership," *Antioch Review* 53 (Fall 1995): 482–93, and Stanley Goldberg, "General Groves and the Atomic West: The Making and the Meaning of Hanford," in *The Atomic West*, ed. Bruce W. Hevly and John M. Findlay (Seattle: University of Washington Press, 1998).

8 The classic work on the Manhattan Project is Richard G. Hewlett and Oscar E. Anderson Jr., *The New World, 1939–1946: A History of the United States Atomic Energy Commission* (University Park: Pennsylvania State University Press, 1962). Richard Rhodes, *The Making of the Atomic Bomb* (New York: Simon and Schuster, 1986), is an excellent account and a great read. F. G. Gosling, *The Manhattan Project: Making the Atomic Bomb* (Washington, D.C.: U.S. Department of Energy, 1994), is a good brief summary.

9 Harry S. Truman, *Memoirs: 1945, Year of Decisions* (Garden City, N.Y.: Doubleday, 1955), 1: 10, 87.

10 Diary of Henry L. Stimson, April 25, 1945, with attached "Memorandum discussed with the President," in *The Manhattan Project: A Documentary Introduction to the Atomic Age*, ed. Michael B. Stoff, Jonathan F. Fanton, and R. Hal Williams (Philadelphia: Temple University Press, 1991), 93–96 (quotations on 95, 96).

11 "Notes of the Interim Committee Meeting," May 31, 1945, in ibid., 117–18.

12 Ibid., 114–15.

13 Ibid., 115.

14 William Lanouette with Bela Silard, *Genius in the Shadows: A Biography of Leo Szilard, the Man behind the Bomb* (New York: Scribner's, 1992), 265.

CHAPTER THREE

1 John W. Dower, *War without Mercy: Race and Power in the Pacific War* (New York: Pantheon, 1986), 10–11. The following discussion of American and Japanese views of one another draws heavily from Dower's seminal work.

2 Ibid., 43–50; Thomas B. Allen and Norman Polmar, *Code-Name Downfall: The Secret Plan to Invade Japan and Why Truman Dropped the Bomb* (New York: Simon and Schuster, 1995), 154–60.

3 Dower, *War without Mercy*, 112.

4 William Manchester, *Goodbye, Darkness: A Memoir of the Pacific War* (Boston: Little, Brown, 1979), 363.

5 Meirion Harries and Susie Harries, *Soldiers of the Sun: The Rise and Fall of the Imperial Japanese Army* (New York: Random House, 1991), 440.

6 Ronald H. Spector, *Eagle against the Sun: The American War with Japan* (New York: Free Press, 1985), 502–3.

7 For a valuable study of the B-29 and its role in the defeat of Japan, see Kenneth P. Werrell, *Blankets of Fire: U.S. Bombers over Japan during World War II* (Washington, D.C.: Smithsonian Institution Press, 1996).

8 Ronald Schaffer, *Wings of Judgment: American Bombing in World War II* (New York: Oxford University Press, 1985), 35–36.

9 Quoted in Michael S. Sherry, *The Rise of American Air Power: The Creation of Armageddon* (New Haven: Yale University Press, 1987), 287.

10 Quoted in Schaffer, *Wings of Judgment*, 128.

11 Quoted in Peter Wyden, *Day One: Before Hiroshima and After* (New York: Simon and Schuster, 1984), 185.

12 Schaffer, *Wings of Judgment*, 132.

13 United States Strategic Bombing Survey, *Japan's Struggle to End the War*, typescript, July 1, 1946, in *The Decision to Drop the Atomic Bomb on Japan*, vol. 1 of *Documentary History of the Truman Presidency*, ed. Dennis Merrill (Bethesda, Md.: University Publications of America, 1995), 376–412.

14 Both quotations are from Daikichi Irokawa, *The Age of Hirohito: In Search of Modern Japan*, trans. Mikiso Hane and John K. Urda (New York: Free Press, 1995), 92.

15 Ibid., 13; Draft Petition from Koichi Kido to Douglas MacArthur, 1948, Box 11 (Kido, Koichi), Subject File, Papers of John G. Brannon, Harry S. Truman Library, Independence, Mo.

16 Quoted in Herbert J. Bix, "Japan's Delayed Surrender: A Reinterpretation," *Diplomatic History* 19 (Spring 1995): 197–225 (quotation on 202).

17 Spector, *Eagle against the Sun*, 532.

18 Quoted in George Feifer, *Tennozan: The Battle of Okinawa and the Atomic Bomb* (New York: Ticknor and Fields, 1992), 278, 286.

19 Quoted in Spector, *Eagle against the Sun*, 537.

20 Ibid., 540; Feifer, *Tennozan*, 484, 528–34.

CHAPTER FOUR

1 *The Entry of the Soviet Union into the War against Japan: Military Plans, 1941–1945* (Washington, D.C.: Department of Defense, 1955), 76–77.

2 Robert H. Ferrell, ed., *Off the Record: The Private Papers of Harry S. Truman* (New York: Harper and Row, 1980), 47.

3 "Minutes of Meeting Held at the White House on Monday, 18 June 1945 at 1530," in *The Decision to Drop the Atomic Bomb on Japan*, vol. 1 of *Documentary History of the Truman Presidency*, ed. Dennis Merrill (Bethesda, Md.: University Publications of America, 1995), 49–93 (quotations on 50, 52).

4 Marshall told Leahy that American casualties during an invasion of Kyushu would not be more than 63,000. See Diary of William D. Leahy, June 18, 1945, Papers of William D. Leahy, Library of Congress, Washington, D.C. See also Barton J. Bernstein, "Compelling Japan's Surrender without the A-Bomb, Soviet Entry, or Invasion: Reconsidering the US Bombing Survey's Early-Surrender Conclusions," *Journal of Strategic Studies* 18 (June 1995): 101–48.

5 Quotation from "Minutes of Meeting Held 18 June 1945," in *Decision to Drop the Atomic Bomb*, ed. Merrill, 54.

6 Ibid., 54, 55.

7 Ibid., 55–57.

8 Ibid., 53.

9 Ibid., 51.

10 Joint War Plans Committee, "Details of the Campaign against Japan" (J.W.P.C. 369/1), June 15, 1945, in Martin J. Sherwin, *A World Destroyed: Hiroshima and Its Legacies*, 3rd ed. (Stanford: Stanford University Press, 2003), 336–45. See also Barton J. Bernstein, "A Postwar Myth: 500,000 U.S. Lives Saved," *Bulletin of the Atomic Scientists* 42 (June/July 1986): 38–40, and Barton J. Bernstein, "Understanding the Atomic Bomb and the Japanese Surrender: Missed Opportunities, Little-Known Near Disasters, and Modern Memory," *Diplomatic History* 19 (Spring 1995): 227–73.

11 A. J. G., Memorandum for the Record, June 18, 1945; J. E. Hull to cincafpac, June 18, 1945; General MacArthur to General Marshall, June 18, 1945; POD 704 TS, Section I, General Records 1945 (Top Secret Correspondence), Office of the Director of Plans and Operations, War Department General Staff, RG 165 (Records of the War Department General and Special Staffs), National Archives, College Park, Md.

12 The question of casualty estimates in the summer of 1945 aroused more in-

tense controversy during the 1990s and early 2000s than any other single issue relating to the use of the atomic bomb. In 1985, Rufus E. Miles Jr. published an article that took issue with the view that the bomb saved staggering numbers of American lives by making an invasion of Japan unnecessary. See Miles, "Hiroshima: The Strange Myth of Half a Million American Lives Saved," *International Security* 10 (Fall 1985): 121–40. The argument he questioned was a staple of the traditional interpretation of Truman's decision to use the bomb. The following year, Barton J. Bernstein, drawing on recently opened documentary evidence, showed that the projected number of deaths reported to Truman at the June 18 meeting fell far short of hundreds of thousands. See Bernstein, "A Postwar Myth," 38–40. John Ray Skates, *The Invasion of Japan: Alternative to the Bomb* (Columbia: University of South Carolina Press, 1994), reached the same conclusion. He argued that the "record does not support the postwar claims of huge Allied casualties to be suffered in the invasion of Japan" (76–82). Revisionist scholars who were critical of Truman's decision cited the new findings as compelling testimony that the use of the atomic bomb was unnecessary.

Traditionalist scholars took sharp exception. Based on the work of Edward J. Drea, *MacArthur's ULTRA: Codebreaking and the War against Japan, 1942–1945* (Lawrence: University Press of Kansas, 1992), they contended that the estimates made in June 1945 were obsolete within a short time. The Japanese buildup of forces on Kyushu was much more rapid and massive than anticipated. In June, Marshall predicted that Japanese defenders on Kyushu would number about 350,000 at the time of the invasion, but by early August the estimated size of enemy forces had already reached nearly 600,000. Thus, traditionalists argued, the casualty estimates in the many hundreds of thousands that Truman and his close advisers cited after the war were credible. See, for example, Robert H. Ferrell, *Harry S. Truman: A Life* (Columbia: University of Missouri Press, 1994); Robert James Maddox, *Weapons for Victory: The Hiroshima Decision Fifty Years Later* (Columbia: University of Missouri Press, 1995); Robert P. Newman, *Truman and the Hiroshima Cult* (East Lansing: Michigan State University Press, 1995); and Thomas B. Allen and Norman Polmar, *Code-Name Downfall: The Secret Plan to Invade Japan and Why Truman Dropped the Bomb* (New York: Simon and Schuster, 1995).

D. M. Giangreco strongly supported the traditional position in articles on the casualty issue. In 1997, he claimed to have demonstrated "the existence and complete acceptance by the War Department and Army of estimates that battle casualties could surpass one million men" in an invasion of Japan. In a later article he suggested that Truman knew about and accepted huge casualty projections in the event of a landing on the Japanese mainland. See Giangreco, "Casualty Projections for U.S. Invasions of Japan, 1945–1946: Planning and Policy Implications," *Journal of Military History* 61 (July 1997):

521–82, and "'A Score of Bloody Okinawas and Iwo Jimas': President Truman and Casualty Estimates for the Invasion of Japan," *Pacific Historical Review* 72 (February 2003): 93–132.

Bernstein vigorously contested Giangreco's arguments. He denied that any primary sources demonstrated that Truman was told by his top advisers in the summer of 1945 that the cost of an invasion of Japan would be several hundreds of thousands of American casualties. He criticized scholars who accepted the postwar casualty claims of Truman and other senior officials as more reliable than contemporary documentary evidence. "There is no 1945 archival evidence supporting Truman's postwar contention," he wrote, "and . . . there is substantial evidence undercutting his claim." See Bernstein, "Reconsidering Truman's Claim of 'Half a Million American Lives' Saved by the Atomic Bomb: The Construction and Deconstruction of a Myth," *Journal of Strategic Studies* 22 (March 1999): 54–95, and "Reconsidering 'Invasion Most Costly': Popular-History Scholarship, Publishing Standards, and the Claim of High U.S. Casualty Estimates to Help Legitimize the Atomic Bombings," *Peace and Change* 24 (April 1999): 220–48.

The debate over casualty estimates was extremely acrimonious, in part because the evidence is neither conclusive nor unassailable. But, as Bernstein pointed out, scholars who claim that Truman's top advisers reported to him that an invasion would exact American casualties in the range of several hundred thousand have neither proven their case nor effectively refuted the evidence that undermines it. The casualty-estimate issue is not of central importance in understanding Truman's decision to drop the bomb. It is probable if not certain that the president would have authorized use of the bomb even if the number of American lives saved was relatively small, at least compared with the figures that he and others cited after the war. One should not lose sight of the fact that the 25,000 deaths that the Joint War Plans Committee estimated for the invasion of Kyushu was a very large number that no policymaker could and no historian should dismiss lightly.

13 Quotation from "Minutes of Meeting Held 18 June 1945," in *Decision to Drop the Atomic Bomb*, ed. Merrill, 54; Conrad C. Crane, *Bombs, Cities, and Civilians: American Airpower Strategy in World War II* (Lawrence: University Press of Kansas, 1993), 136–37; Richard B. Frank, "Ketsu Go, Downfall, and Ending the War: Japanese and American Political and Military Strategy in 1945," forthcoming in *Nuclear Energy and the Legacy of Harry S. Truman*, ed. J. Samuel Walker (Kirksville, Mo.: Truman State University Press, 2016); Charles F. Brower, *Defeating Japan: The Joint Chiefs of Staff and Strategy in the Pacific War, 1943–1945* (New York: Palgrave Macmillan, 2012).

14 Quoted in Ronald Schaffer, *Wings of Judgment: American Bombing in World War II* (New York: Oxford University Press, 1985), 138.

15 Joint Intelligence Committee, "Defeat of Japan by Blockade and Bombard-

ment" (J.I.C. 266/1), April 18, 1945, CCS 381 Japan (4-6-45), Geographic File, RG 218 (Records of the U.S. Joint Chiefs of Staff), National Archives.

16 Larry I. Bland and Sharon Ritenour Stevens, eds., *The Papers of George Catlett Marshall* (Baltimore: Johns Hopkins University Press, 1996), 4: 592.

17 "Minutes of Meeting Held by the Joint Chiefs of Staff and Heads of Civilian War Agencies," May 22, 1945, CCS 334 Chiefs of Staff (2-2-45), Central Decimal File, 1942–45, RG 218, National Archives; Frank, "Ketsu Go, Downfall, and Ending the War"; Brower, *Defeating Japan* (King quotation on p. 10). See also Leahy Diary, May 15, 1945, Leahy Papers.

18 G. C. Marshall to the Secretary of War, with enclosed memorandum, June 4, 1945, in Sherwin, *A World Destroyed*, 353–55 (quotation on 355).

19 "Minutes of Meeting Held 18 June 1945," in *Decision to Drop the Atomic Bomb*, ed. Merrill, 55, 56.

20 Quoted in Leon V. Sigal, *Fighting to a Finish: The Politics of War Termination in the United States and Japan, 1945* (Ithaca: Cornell University Press, 1988), 97.

21 Quoted in Gerhard L. Weinberg, *A World at Arms: A Global History of World War II* (New York: Cambridge University Press, 1994), 439.

22 Quoted in Newman, *Truman and the Hiroshima Cult*, 61.

23 Quoted in Gar Alperovitz, *The Decision to Use the Atomic Bomb and the Architecture of an American Myth* (New York: Alfred A. Knopf, 1995), 38.

24 Ibid., 45–46.

25 Diary of Henry L. Stimson, July 2, 1945, with attached Memorandum for the President, in *The Manhattan Project: A Documentary Introduction to the Atomic Age*, ed. Michael B. Stoff, Jonathan F. Fanton, and R. Hal Williams (Philadelphia: Temple University Press, 1991), 164–70 (quotations on 166, 169, 170).

26 Quoted in Sigal, *Fighting to a Finish*, 73.

27 *Foreign Relations of the United States, Diplomatic Papers: The Conference of Berlin (The Potsdam Conference) 1945* (Washington, D.C.: Government Printing Office, 1960), 2: 1267–71; Henry L. Stimson and McGeorge Bundy, *On Active Service in Peace and War* (New York: Harper and Brothers, 1947), 628.

28 George C. Marshall to the Secretary of War, June 9, 1945; Marshall to the Secretary of War, June 15, 1945, with attached "Memorandum of Comments on 'Ending the Japanese War,'" June 14, 1945; Joseph C. Grew, Memorandum for the President, June 13, 1945; Safe File (Japan after Dec 7/41), RG 107 (Records of the Office of the Secretary of War), National Archives.

29 Office of War Information, Domestic Radio Bureau, "Japan's Unconditional Surrender," [June 1945], Official File 197 (Misc. 1945–46), Harry S. Truman Papers, Harry S. Truman Library, Independence, Mo.

30 The polls are cited in Sigal, *Fighting to a Finish*, 95.

31 Gar Alperovitz has shown that the policy of unconditional surrender was not unchallenged in the United States; he points out that Truman and Byrnes did

not face "an unyielding wall of public opinion demanding rigid allegiance to 'unconditional surrender'" (Alperovitz, *Decision to Use the Atomic Bomb*, 223–32). Some newspapers and magazines and even some leading Republicans urged Truman to moderate the policy, or at least clarify what it meant, as a means of speeding the end of the war. Alperovitz makes an important point, but polls at the time suggested that Truman would have been taking a considerable risk by electing to change the policy. For a president who was still insecure in his position, unsure of his public standing, committed to carrying out Roosevelt's legacy, and, most importantly, seeking a way to end the war decisively at the lowest possible cost in American lives, the potential drawbacks of softening the demand for unconditional surrender had to be balanced against the potential (but far from certain) benefits.

32 MAGIC—Diplomatic Summary, No. 1205, July 13, 1945, MAGIC Diplomatic Summaries 1942–1945, Record Group 457 (Records of the National Security Agency/Central Security Service), National Archives.

33 John Weckerling to the Deputy Chief of Staff, July 13, 1945, Army-Operations, OPD Executive File #17, Item 13, RG 165, National Archives. A copy of this document is available in Reel 109, Item 2581, Marshall Foundation National Archives Project, George C. Marshall Papers, George C. Marshall Library, Lexington, Va. For Weckerling's background, see *Generals of the Army*, February 1953, in Box 6 (Weckerling, John), Papers of Dale M. Hellegers, Truman Library.

34 *Foreign Relations of the U.S.: Potsdam*, 1: 877–88.

35 Daikichi Irokawa, *The Age of Hirohito*, trans. Mikiso Hane and John K. Urda (New York: Free Press, 1995), 34, 92.

36 J. J. McCloy, "Memorandum of Conversation with General Marshall," May 29, 1945, Safe File (S-1), RG 107, National Archives.

37 Richard G. Hewlett and Oscar E. Anderson Jr., *The New World, 1939–1946: A History of the United States Atomic Energy Commission* (University Park: Pennsylvania State University Press, 1962), 358.

38 "Notes of the Interim Committee Meeting, May 31, 1945," in *Manhattan Project*, ed. Stoff, Fanton, and Williams, 117. Some scientists did not agree with their colleagues who advised the Interim Committee on this issue. Spurred by the irrepressible Leo Szilard, a group of seven Manhattan Project scientists took a different position in a document known as the Franck Report, named after physicist James Franck, who chaired the committee that prepared it. The Franck Report urged a demonstration of the bomb in the desert or on an isolated island. It suggested that an "unannounced attack" on Japan would "sacrifice public support throughout the world, precipitate the race for armaments, and prejudice the possibility of reaching an international agreement on the future control of [atomic] weapons." The report did not reach top policymakers, and it failed to persuade Oppenheimer and other

members of the Scientific Panel advising the Interim Committee. The Franck Report appears in Sherwin, *A World Destroyed*, 323–33.

CHAPTER FIVE

1 Robert H. Ferrell, ed., *Off the Record: The Private Papers of Harry S. Truman* (New York: Harper and Row, 1980), 49; Robert H. Ferrell, ed., *Dear Bess: The Letters from Harry to Bess Truman, 1910–1959* (New York: W. W. Norton, 1983), 517–18. Stalin had recently assumed the title "Generalissimo."

2 Ferrell, *Dear Bess*, 516.

3 Quoted in Gar Alperovitz, *The Decision to Use the Atomic Bomb and the Architecture of an American Myth* (New York: Alfred A. Knopf, 1995), 148–49.

4 Quoted in Richard Rhodes, *The Making of the Atomic Bomb* (New York: Simon and Schuster, 1986), 666.

5 Quoted in ibid., 673, 675. See also Ferenc Morton Szasz, *The Day the Sun Rose Twice: The Story of the Trinity Site Nuclear Explosion, July 16, 1945* (Albuquerque: University of New Mexico Press, 1984), 79–91.

6 Interim Committee Log, July 16, 1945, War Department Message from Harrison to Stimson, July 16, 1945, in *The Manhattan Project: A Documentary Introduction to the Atomic Age*, ed. Michael B. Stoff, Jonathan F. Fanton, and R. Hal Williams (Philadelphia: Temple University Press, 1991), 183; Stimson's Notes for His Diary, July 16, 1945, ibid., 184.

7 Ferrell, *Off the Record*, 53. Truman met Churchill for the first time on July 16, and wrote in his diary that they "had a most pleasant conversation." He added that Churchill gave him "a lot of hooey" but thought they could "get along if he doesn't give me too much soft soap." Ibid., 51.

8 Ferrell, *Dear Bess*, 519.

9 For a clear statement of this position and a sharp dissent, see Gar Alperovitz and Robert L. Messer, and Barton J. Bernstein, "Correspondence: Marshall, Truman, and the Decision to Drop the Bomb," *International Security* 16 (Winter 1991/92): 204–21. For an elaboration of Bernstein's views, see his "Understanding the Atomic Bomb and the Japanese Surrender: Missed Opportunities, Little-Known Near Disasters, and Modern Memory," *Diplomatic History* 19 (Spring 1995): 227–73.

10 Ferrell, *Dear Bess*, 519–20; *Foreign Relations of the United States, Diplomatic Papers: The Conference of Berlin (The Potsdam Conference), 1945* (Washington, D.C.: Government Printing Office, 1960), 2: 52–63, 116–30.

11 Stimson Notes for His Diary, July 21, 1945, in *Manhattan Project*, ed. Stoff, Fanton, and Williams, 203.

12 L. R. Groves, Memorandum for the Secretary of War, July 18, 1945, in *The Decision to Drop the Atomic Bomb on Japan*, vol. 1 of *Documentary History of the Truman Presidency*, ed. Dennis Merrill (Bethesda, Md.: University Publications of America, 1995), 122–35 (quotations on 122, 130–31).

13 Stimson Notes for His Diary, July 21, 1945, in *Manhattan Project*, ed. Stoff, Fanton, and Williams, 203–4.

14 Ferrell, *Off the Record*, 54, 55, 56.

15 John N. Stone, Memorandum for General Arnold, July 24, 1945, in *Decision to Drop the Atomic Bomb*, ed. Merrill, 151–54; Thomas T. Handy to Carl Spaatz, July 25, 1945, Marshall Foundation National Archives Project, Xerox 1482-175, George C. Marshall Library, Lexington, Va. See also the discussion in Robert James Maddox, *Weapons for Victory: The Hiroshima Decision Fifty Years Later* (Columbia: University of Missouri Press, 1995), 104–8.

David McCullough, in *Truman* (New York: Simon and Schuster, 1992), shows a photograph of a document that he claims was Truman's order to drop the bomb (photograph number 10 following page 288). The document McCullough exhibits, however, was actually an authorization to issue a *press release* about the bomb at the appropriate time. See Incoming Message to the President from the Secretary of War, No. 41011, July 30, 1945, and Truman's handwritten response, in *Decision to Drop the Atomic Bomb*, ed. Merrill, 174–75.

16 Stimson Notes for His Diary, July 24, 1945, in *Manhattan Project*, ed. Stoff, Fanton, and Williams, 212–14; Ferrell, *Off the Record*, 55–56.

17 Barton J. Bernstein, "The Struggle over History: Defining the Hiroshima Narrative," in *Judgment at the Smithsonian: The Bombing of Hiroshima and Nagasaki*, ed. Philip Nobile (New York: Marlowe, 1995), 177.

18 Stimson Notes for His Diary, July 23, 1945, in *Manhattan Project*, ed. Stoff, Fanton, and Williams, 210.

19 *Foreign Relations of the U.S.: Potsdam*, 2: 203–25.

20 Stimson Notes for His Diary, July 23, 1945, in *Manhattan Project*, ed. Stoff, Fanton, and Williams, 209–10.

21 Robert L. Messer, *The End of an Alliance: James F. Byrnes, Roosevelt, Truman, and the Origins of the Cold War* (Chapel Hill: University of North Carolina Press, 1982), 94.

22 Joseph E. Davies Journal, July 28, 1945, Davies Diary, July 29, 1945, Chronological File, Joseph E. Davies Papers, Library of Congress, Washington, D.C.

23 William D. Leahy Diary, July 17, 1945, William D. Leahy Papers, Library of Congress, Washington, D.C.

24 Walter Brown Notes, July 24, 1945, Box 2, Series 5 (State Department), James F. Byrnes Papers, Special Collections, Robert Muldrow Cooper Library, Clemson University, Clemson, S.C.

25 Stimson Notes for His Diary, July 23, 1945, in *Manhattan Project*, ed. Stoff, Fanton, and Williams, 210–11.

26 G. C. Marshall, Memorandum for the President, July 26, 1945, Folder 38, Box 81, George C. Marshall Papers, Marshall Library.

27 Ferrell, *Dear Bess*, 522.

28 Ferrell, *Off the Record*, 57–58.

29 Harry S. Truman, *Memoirs: 1945, Year of Decisions* (Garden City, N.Y.: Double-day, 1955), 1: 416. Stalin's interpreter recalled that the Soviet leader made no verbal reply but only nodded his head in acknowledgment. See David Holloway, *Stalin and the Bomb: The Soviet Union and Atomic Energy, 1939–1956* (New Haven: Yale University Press, 1994), 117.

30 David Holloway, "Jockeying for Position in the Postwar World: Soviet Entry into the War with Japan in August 1945," in *The End of the Pacific War: Reap-praisals*, ed. Tsuyoshi Hasegawa (Stanford: Stanford University Press, 2007), 145–88. On Soviet espionage and its contribution to the building of the Soviet bomb, see Richard Rhodes, *Dark Sun: The Making of the Hydrogen Bomb* (New York: Simon and Schuster, 1995), 82–179.

31 Ferrell, *Dear Bess*, 521.

32 Handy to Spaatz, July 25, 1945, Marshall Library.

33 Fred M. Vinson, Cable to the President (MR-OUT-203), n.d., Berlin Confer-ence (Communications from Map Room), Naval Aide Files; Vinson Memo-randum for the President, July 20, 1945, General File, Box 140, President's Secretary's Files, Harry S. Truman Papers, Harry S. Truman Library, Inde-pendence, Mo.

34 G. C. Marshall, Memorandum for the President, n.d., Folder 39, Box 81, Mar-shall Papers; Marshall, Memorandum for the Secretary of War, August 1, 1945, Folder 30, Box 84, Marshall Papers; Message from Tripartite Conference to agwar, victory-out-346, July 26, 1945, Verifax 2726, Item 2589, Marshall Foundation National Archives Project, Marshall Library; Marshall Report on "Japanese Capitulation," n.d., Subject File—Cabinet (War, Secy of), Box 157, President's Secretary's File, Truman Papers.

35 George A. Lincoln, "Military Use of the Atomic Bomb," n.d., 33–40, copy in Vertical File (Atomic Bomb—Ethical Aspects), Truman Library. The origi-nal copy of this report is in the George A. Lincoln Papers at the U.S. Military Academy, West Point, N.Y.

36 Stimson Diary entry, June 19, 1945, in *Manhattan Project*, ed. Stoff, Fanton, and Williams, 155.

37 *Foreign Relations of the U.S.: Potsdam*, 1: 887, 888.

38 Henry L. Stimson to the President, July 2, 1945, with attached draft "Procla-mation by the Heads of State," in *Decision to Drop the Atomic Bomb*, ed. Merrill, 102–5.

39 *Foreign Relations of the U.S.: Potsdam*, 2: 1268–69.

40 Ferrell, *Off the Record*, 56.

41 For a discussion of the Zacharias broadcast, see Alperovitz, *Decision to Use the Atomic Bomb*, 394–99.

42 "Proclamation Defining Terms for the Japanese Surrender," July 26, 1945, in *Manhattan Project*, ed. Stoff, Fanton, and Williams, 215–16.

43 Quoted in Robert J. C. Butow, *Japan's Decision to Surrender* (Stanford: Stanford University Press, 1954), 145, 148.

44 Department of the Army, *Army Battle Casualties and Nonbattle Deaths in World War II: Final Report* (1953), p. 100, copy available in Modern Military Branch, National Archives.

45 For the story of the *Indianapolis*, see Dan Kurtzman, *Fatal Voyage: The Sinking of the USS Indianapolis* (New York: Pocket, 1990), and Stanley Weintraub, *The Last Great Victory: The End of World War II, July/August 1945* (New York: Dutton, 1995).

CHAPTER SIX

1 Richard Rhodes, *The Making of the Atomic Bomb* (New York: Simon and Schuster, 1986), 709, 710, 711; Telecon Message FN-08-21—Subject: Hiroshima Mission, August 8, 1945, Chronological Correspondence, Box 5, Papers of H. H. Arnold, Library of Congress, Washington, D.C.

2 Rhodes, *Making of the Atomic Bomb*, 714–34 (quotation on 718); United States Strategic Bombing Survey, *The Effects of Atomic Bombs on Hiroshima and Nagasaki* (1946), in *The Decision to Drop the Atomic Bomb on Japan*, vol. 1 of *Documentary History of the Truman Presidency*, ed. Dennis Merrill (Bethesda, Md.: University Publications of America, 1995), 313–28; Committee for the Compilation of Materials on Damage Caused by the Atomic Bombs in Hiroshima and Nagasaki, *Hiroshima and Nagasaki: The Physical, Medical, and Social Effects of the Atomic Bombings*, trans. Eisei Ishikawa and David L. Swain (New York: Basic Books, 1981), 352–67; Joint Chiefs of Staff, "Effects of Atomic Bombs on Hiroshima and Nagasaki" (J.C.S. 1501/3), May 20, 1946, Section 3-A, ABC File 471.6 Atom (17 Aug 45), Office of the Director of Plans and Operations, RG 165 (Records of the War Department General and Special Staffs), National Archives, College Park, Md.

3 Harry S. Truman, *Memoirs: 1945, Year of Decisions* (Garden City, N.Y.: Doubleday, 1955), 1: 421; David McCullough, *Truman* (New York: Simon and Schuster, 1992), 454–55.

4 "Statement by the President of the United States," [August 6, 1945], in *Decision to Drop the Atomic Bomb*, ed. Merrill, 196, 197, 198.

5 The text of the leaflets appears in *Decision to Drop the Atomic Bomb*, ed. Merrill, 194–95.

6 United States Strategic Bombing Survey, *The Effects of Atomic Bombs*, in *Decision to Drop the Atomic Bomb*, ed. Merrill, 319–33; Committee for the Compilation of Materials on Damage Caused by the Atomic Bombs, *Hiroshima and Nagasaki*, 353, 367; Rhodes, *Making of the Atomic Bomb*, 737–42.

7 Strategic Bombing Survey, *Effects of Atomic Bombs*, in *Decision to Drop the Atomic Bomb*, ed. Merrill, 325–30; Committee for the Compilation of Materials on Damage Caused by the Atomic Bombs, *Hiroshima and Nagasaki*,

21–29, 67–80; Radiation Effects Research Foundation, "Frequently Asked Questions" (http://www.rerf.jp/general/qa_e/qa2.html), "Solid Cancer Risks among Atomic Bomb Survivors" (http://www.rerf.jp/radefx/late_e/cancrisk.html), "Leukemia Risks among Atomic-Bomb Survivors" (http.rerf.jp/radefx/late_e/leukemia.html), and "RERF's Views on Residual Radiation" (December 8, 2012, http://www.rerf.jp/news/pdf/residualrad_ps_e.pdf), all accessed April 30, 2015; Paul Ham, "Why Americans Have Been Duped over the Use of the Atomic Bomb," November 9, 2014, http://historynewsnetwork.org/article/157392 (accessed November 10, 2014).

8 Quoted in Paul Boyer, *By the Bomb's Early Light: American Thought and Culture at the Dawn of the Atomic Age* (New York: Pantheon, 1985), 5.

9 David Holloway, *Stalin and the Bomb: The Soviet Union and Atomic Energy, 1939–1956* (New Haven: Yale University Press, 1994), 127–33 (quotation on 132).

10 Quoted in Robert J. C. Butow, *Japan's Decision to Surrender* (Stanford: Stanford University Press, 1954), 151.

11 Walter Brown Notes, July 18, 1945, Box 2, Series 5 (State Department), James F. Byrnes Papers, Special Collections, Robert Muldrow Cooper Library, Clemson University, Clemson, S.C.; Tsuyoshi Hasegawa, *Racing the Enemy: Stalin, Truman, and the Surrender of Japan* (Cambridge: Harvard University Press, 2005), chap. 5; Tsuyoshi Hasegawa, "The Atomic Bombs and Soviet Entry into the War against Japan: Which Was More Important in Japan's Decision to Surrender in the Pacific War?," in *The End of the Pacific War: Reappraisals*, ed. Tsuyoshi Hasegawa (Stanford: Stanford University Press, 2007), 113–44.

12 For a discussion of "Kido's and the emperor's concern over growing popular criticism of the throne and its occupant," see Herbert P. Bix, *Hirohito and the Making of Modern Japan* (New York: HarperCollins, 2000), 511, and Herbert P. Bix, "Japan's Delayed Surrender: A Reinterpretation," *Diplomatic History* 19 (Spring 1995): 197–225.

13 Koichi Kido, Draft Petition to Douglas MacArthur, 1948, Box 11 (Kido, Koichi), Subject File, Papers of John G. Brannon, Harry S. Truman Library, Independence, Mo.; Bix, *Hirohito*, 511–17; Hasegawa, *Racing the Enemy*, chap. 5; Richard B. Frank, *Downfall: The End of the Imperial Japanese Empire* (New York: Random House, 1999), 290–96.

14 Sadao Asada, "The Shock of the Atomic Bomb and Japan's Decision to Surrender: A Reconsideration," *Pacific Historical Review* 67 (November 1998): 477–512.

15 Note from the Swiss chargé d'affaires ad interim to the Secretary of State, August 10, 1945, in *The Manhattan Project: A Documentary Introduction to the Atomic Age*, ed. Michael B. Stoff, Jonathan F. Fanton, and R. Hal Williams (Philadelphia: Temple University Press, 1991), 246.

16 Brown Notes, August 10, 1945, Byrnes Papers; Hasegawa, *Racing the Enemy*,
    218–19; Hal Brands, "Who Saved the Emperor? The MacArthur Myth and
    U.S. Policy toward Hirohito and the Japanese Imperial Institution, 1942–
    1946," *Pacific Historical Review* 75 (May 2006): 271–305.

17 Note from the Secretary of State to the Swiss chargé d'affaires ad interim,
    August 11, 1945, in *Manhattan Project*, ed. Stoff, Fanton, and Williams, 247.

18 Telecon Message FN-08-21, August 8, 1945, Arnold Papers (see note 1 above).

19 Henry A. Wallace Diary, August 10, 1945, in *The Price of Vision: The Diary
    of Henry A. Wallace, 1942–1946*, ed. John Morton Blum (Boston: Houghton
    Mifflin, 1973), 474.

20 Quoted in Butow, *Japan's Decision to Surrender*, 207.

21 Ibid., 213.

22 Ibid., 2, 3.

23 Hasegawa, *Racing the Enemy*, chap. 5; Bix, *Hirohito*, 523; Bix, "Japan's Delayed
    Surrender," 218; Asada, "Shock of the Atomic Bomb," 491–92, 505–8.

24 Richard B. Frank, "Ketsu Go, Downfall, and Ending the War: Japanese and
    American Political and Military Strategy in 1945," forthcoming in *Nuclear
    Energy and the Legacy of Harry S. Truman*, ed. J. Samuel Walker (Kirksville,
    Mo.: Truman State University Press, 2016); Richard B. Frank, "The Bomb's
    Long Aftermath," *Wartime*, no. 61 (September 2013): 16–21; Sumio Hatano,
    "The Atomic Bomb and Soviet Entry into the War: Of Equal Importance,"
    in *The End of the Pacific War*, ed. Hasegawa, 95–112; Gerhard L. Weinberg,
    A World at Arms: A Global History of World War II (New York: Cambridge
    University Press, 1994), 892.

25 For a thoughtful and, in my judgment, persuasive analysis of the likelihood
    that the war would have ended without the bomb and before an invasion,
    see Barton J. Bernstein, "Understanding the Atomic Bomb and the Japanese
    Surrender: Missed Opportunities, Little-Known Near Disasters, and Mod-
    ern Memory," *Diplomatic History* 19 (Spring 1995): 227–73. He suggests that
    "it is *likely, but far from definite*, that a combination of non-nuclear options
    could have ended the war in the summer without the atomic bombings"
    (228, emphasis in original). Hasegawa argues that even without the use of
    the bomb, "the war would have ended shortly after Soviet entry into the
    war, almost certainly before November 1" ("The Atomic Bombs and Soviet
    Entry into the War against Japan," 46). Richard Frank is less certain that the
    war would have ended before an invasion in the absence of the atomic bomb,
    but he makes a strong case that the destruction of railroads would have led
    to severe food shortages and growing discontent among the Japanese people.
    See Frank, *Downfall*, 352–54.

26 On this point, see Gar Alperovitz, *The Decision to Use the Atomic Bomb and the
    Architecture of an American Myth* (New York: Alfred A. Knopf, 1995), 329–65.

27 Herbert Feis, *The Atomic Bomb and the End of World War II* (Princeton: Princeton University Press, 1966), 191.

28 William D. Leahy, *I Was There: The Personal Story of the Chief of Staff to Presidents Roosevelt and Truman Based on His Notes and Diaries Made at the Time* (New York: Whittlesey House, 1950), 441.

29 Barton J. Bernstein, "Ike and Hiroshima: Did He Oppose It?," *Journal of Strategic Studies* 10 (September 1987): 377–89.

30 G. C. Marshall to the Secretary of War, with enclosed memorandum, June 4, 1945, in Martin J. Sherwin, *A World Destroyed: Hiroshima and Its Legacies*, 3rd ed. (Stanford: Stanford University Press, 2003), 355.

31 "Minutes of Meeting Held 18 June 1945," in *Decision to Drop the Atomic Bomb*, ed. Merrill, 52.

32 Quoted in Alperovitz, *Decision to Use the Atomic Bomb*, 359.

33 Quoted in Stanley Weintraub, *The Last Great Victory: The End of World War II, July/August 1945* (New York: Dutton, 1995), 229.

34 Robert H. Ferrell, ed., *Off the Record: The Private Papers of Harry S. Truman* (New York: Harper and Row, 1980), 53–54; Barton J. Bernstein, "The Alarming Japanese Buildup on Southern Kyushu, Growing U.S. Fears, and Counterfactual Analysis: Would the Planned November 1945 of Southern Kyushu Have Occurred?," *Pacific Historical Review* 68 (November 1999): 561–609.

35 Some scholars have suggested that the use of the bomb saved not only American lives but also large numbers of Japanese lives. The continuation of B-29 raids, the effects of the blockade, and if it became necessary, the carnage of an invasion would have caused more deaths than the attacks on Hiroshima and Nagasaki. On this point, see Robert P. Newman, *Truman and the Hiroshima Cult* (East Lansing: Michigan State University Press, 1995), 187–88, and Thomas B. Allen and Norman Polmar, *Code-Name Downfall: The Secret Plan to Invade Japan and Why Truman Dropped the Bomb* (New York: Simon and Schuster, 1995), 293. This might well be true, but it was not a consideration for Truman and his advisers. General LeMay commented late in his life that although the bomb probably saved the lives of many Japanese, "we didn't give a damn about them at the time." Quoted in Alperovitz, *Decision to Use the Atomic Bomb*, 341.

36 *New York Times*, August 10, 1945, 12; Message to the Men and Woman of the Manhattan Project, August 9, 1945, Official File 692-A, Harry S. Truman Papers, Truman Library.

37 Brown Notes, August 6, 1945, Byrnes Papers; Stanley Goldberg, "Racing to the Finish: The Decision to Bomb Hiroshima and Nagasaki," *Journal of American–East Asian Relations* 4 (Summer 1995): 117–28; Robert S. Norris, *Racing for the Bomb: General Leslie R. Groves, The Manhattan Project's Indispensable Man* (South Royalton, Vt.: Steerforth Press, 2002), 377.

38 Henry L. Stimson, "The Decision to Use the Atomic Bomb," *Harper's Magazine* 194 (February 1947): 97–107 (quotation on 106).

39 Barton J. Bernstein, "Roosevelt, Truman and the Atomic Bomb, 1941–1945: A Reinterpretation," *Political Science Quarterly* 90 (Spring 1975): 23–69.

40 Curtis E. LeMay with MacKinlay Kantor, *Mission with LeMay: My Story* (Garden City, N.Y.: Doubleday, 1965), 383.

41 Samuel McCrea Cavert to Harry S. Truman, August 9, 1945, and Truman to Cavert, August 11, 1945, both in *Decision to Drop the Atomic Bomb*, ed. Merrill, 213–14.

CHAPTER SEVEN

1 Michael J. Yavenditti, "The American People and the Use of Atomic Bombs on Japan: The 1940s," *Historian* 36 (February 1974): 224–47.

2 Norman Cousins and Thomas K. Finletter, "A Beginning for Sanity," *Saturday Review of Literature* 29 (June 15, 1946): 5–9; John Hersey, "Hiroshima," *New Yorker*, August 31, 1946, 15–26. Hersey's article was soon published as a book, *Hiroshima* (New York: Alfred A. Knopf, 1946).

3 United States Strategic Bombing Survey, *Summary Report (Pacific War)*, July 1, 1946, in *The Decision to Drop the Atomic Bomb on Japan*, vol. 1 of *Documentary History of the Truman Presidency*, ed. Dennis Merrill (Bethesda, Md.: University Publications of America, 1995), 413–46 (quotation on 440).

4 For critiques of the conclusion of the Strategic Bombing Survey regarding the end of the war, see Robert P. Newman, *Truman and the Hiroshima Cult* (East Lansing: Michigan State University Press, 1995), 33–56; Barton J. Bernstein, "Compelling Japan's Surrender without the A-Bomb, Soviet Entry, or Invasion: Reconsidering the US Bombing Survey's Early-Surrender Conclusions," *Journal of Strategic Studies* 18 (June 1995): 101–48; and Gian P. Gentile, *How Effective Is Strategic Bombing? Lessons Learned from World War II to Kosovo* (New York: New York University Press, 2001).

    Another official study suggested that neither the bomb nor an invasion was needed to end the war, though this one was never published. A report prepared by Army Intelligence in early 1946 contended that the Soviet invasion of Manchuria would have brought about the Japanese surrender and that the chances an American invasion of Kyushu would have been necessary were "remote." The sources used by the authors of this document are unclear, but the conclusion that Soviet entry into the war would have persuaded the Japanese to surrender was inconsistent with the analysis of military planners in the summer of 1945. See R. F. Ennis, Memorandum for Chief, Strategic Policy Section, S & P Group, OPD, April 30, 1946, Section 7, ABC File 471.6 Atom (17 Aug 45), Office of the Director of Plans and Operations, RG 165 (Records of the War Department General and Special Staffs), National Archives, College Park, Md.

5   Notes of Interim Committee Meeting, May 31, 1945, in *The Manhattan Project: A Documentary Introduction to the Atomic Age*, ed. Michael B. Stoff, Jonathan B. Fanton, and R. Hal Williams (Philadelphia: Temple University Press, 1991), 117.

6   Quoted in Martin J. Sherwin, *A World Destroyed: Hiroshima and Its Legacies*, 3rd ed. (Stanford: Stanford University Press, 2003), 200.

7   Quoted in James G. Hershberg, *James B. Conant: Harvard to Hiroshima and the Making of the Nuclear Age* (New York: Alfred A. Knopf, 1993), 229. On scientists and the use of the bomb as a means of encouraging international cooperation, see also Barton J. Bernstein, "Four Physicists and the Bomb: The Early Years, 1945–1950," *Historical Studies in the Physical and Biological Sciences* 18 (1988): 231–63, and Peter Wyden, *Day One: Before Hiroshima and After* (New York: Simon and Schuster, 1984), 148, 178.

8   On Conant's concerns about the effects of criticism of the use of atomic bombs, see Hershberg, *James B. Conant*, 279–304 (quotation on 293–94), and Barton J. Bernstein, "Seizing the Contested Terrain of Early Nuclear History: Stimson, Conant, and Their Allies Explain the Decision to Use the Atomic Bomb," *Diplomatic History* 17 (Winter 1993): 35–72.

9   Henry L. Stimson, "The Decision to Use the Atomic Bomb," *Harper's Magazine* 194 (February 1947): 97–107 (quotations on 102, 107).

10 For Bundy's recollections of the source of the casualty estimate, see Gar Alperovitz, *The Decision to Use the Atomic Bomb and the Architecture of an American Myth* (New York: Alfred A. Knopf, 1995), 468. Bundy provided a thoughtful analysis of the reasons for dropping the bomb in a book he published in 1988, more than 40 years after he served as the "scribe" for Stimson's *Harper's Magazine* article. He emphasized that Truman, Stimson, and other policymakers were primarily interested in the bomb as a way to end the war at the earliest possible moment, and he dismissed the view that their foremost concern was to impress the Soviets with it. Bundy did not, however, simply reiterate the points that Stimson (and he) had made in 1947. He acknowledged that the use of the bomb had not received as much high-level consideration as Stimson's article had suggested and that "revisionist scholars are on strong ground when they question flat assertions that the bomb saved a million lives." See Bundy, *Danger and Survival: Choices about the Bomb in the First Fifty Years* (New York: Random House, 1988), 54–97, 647 n. 19.

11 Barton J. Bernstein, "Writing, Righting, or Wronging the Historical Record: President Truman's Letter on His Atomic-Bomb Decision," *Diplomatic History* 16 (Winter 1992): 163–73.

12 Harry S. Truman to Roman Bohnen, December 12, 1946, and Truman to Irv Kupcinet, August 5, 1963, in *Decision to Drop the Atomic Bomb*, ed. Merrill, 449, 553; Harry S. Truman, *Memoirs: 1945, Year of Decisions* (Garden City, N.Y.: Doubleday, 1955), 1: 417; Alperovitz, *Decision to Use the Atomic Bomb*, 516–17.

13 U.S. Senate, Special Committee on Atomic Energy, *Hearings on Atomic Energy*, 79th Cong., 1st Sess., 1946, Part 1, 38–39; Winston S. Churchill, *Triumph and Tragedy*, vol. 6 of *The Second World War* (Boston: Houghton Mifflin, 1953), 552; John P. Sutherland, "The Story Gen. Marshall Told Me," *U.S. News and World Report* 47 (November 2, 1959): 50–56; *New York Times*, August 30, 1945, 1.

14 Herbert Feis, *Japan Subdued: The Atomic Bomb and the End of the War in the Pacific* (Princeton: Princeton University Press, 1961), 11–12, 178–87.

15 Gar Alperovitz, *Atomic Diplomacy: Hiroshima and Potsdam* (New York: Simon and Schuster, 1965).

16 For detailed reviews of the historiographical debates over the use of the bomb, see Barton J. Bernstein, "The Atomic Bomb and American Foreign Policy, 1941–1945: An Historiographical Controversy," *Peace and Change* 2 (Spring 1974): 1–16; Barton J. Bernstein, "The Struggle over History: Defining the Hiroshima Narrative," in *Judgment at the Smithsonian: The Bombing of Hiroshima and Nagasaki*, ed. Philip Nobile (New York: Marlowe, 1995), 127–256; Barton J. Bernstein, "Introducing the Interpretive Problems of Japan's 1945 Surrender: A Historiographical Essay on Recent Literature in the West," in *The End of the Pacific War: Reappraisals*, ed. Tsuyoshi Hasegawa (Stanford: Stanford University Press, 2007), 9–64; Michael Kort, "The Historiography of Hiroshima: The Rise and Fall of Revisionism," *New England Journal of History* 64 (Fall 2007): 31–48; J. Samuel Walker, "The Decision to Use the Bomb: A Historiographical Update," in *Hiroshima in History and Memory*, ed. Michael J. Hogan (New York: Cambridge University Press, 1996), 11–37; J. Samuel Walker, "Recent Literature on Truman's Atomic Bomb Decision: A Search for Middle Ground," *Diplomatic History* 29 (April 2005): 311–34, and an updated version, "Recent Literature on Truman's Atomic Bomb Decision: The Triumph of the Middle Ground?," in *America in the World: The Historiography of American Foreign Relations since 1941*, ed. Frank Costigliola and Michael J. Hogan, 2nd ed. (New York: Cambridge University Press, 2014), 83–104.

17 Walker, "The Decision to Use the Bomb," 18–32.

18 *Wall Street Journal*, August 29, 1994, A10; Michael J. Hogan, "The Enola Gay Controversy: History, Memory, and the Politics of Presentation," in Hogan, *Hiroshima in History and Memory*, 200–232.

19 The exhibit label quoted appeared under the title "August 6, 1945." For insightful works on the *Enola Gay* exhibit, see Hogan, "The Enola Gay Controversy," in *Hiroshima in History and Memory*, ed. Hogan, 200–232; Bernstein, "The Struggle over History," in *Judgment at the Smithsonian*, ed. Nobile, 202–40; five articles that appeared in *Journal of American History* 82 (December 1995): Richard H. Kohn, "History and the Culture Wars: The Case of the Smithsonian's *Enola Gay* Exhibition" (1036–63), Martin Harwit, "Academic

Freedom in 'The Last Act'" (1064–82), Martin J. Sherwin, "Hiroshima as Politics and History" (1085–93), Edward T. Linenthal, "Struggling with History and Memory" (1094–1101), and John W. Dower, "Triumphal and Tragic Narratives of the War in Asia" (1124–35); Tony Capaccio and Uday Mohan, "Missing the Target," *American Journalism Review* 17 (July/August 1995): 18–26; Edward T. Linenthal and Tom Engelhardt, eds., *History Wars: The "Enola Gay" and Other Battles for the American Past* (New York: Metropolitan Books, 1996); Martin Harwit, *An Exhibit Denied: Lobbying the History of "Enola Gay"* (New York: Copernicus, 1996); four articles that appeared in *Technology and Culture* 39 (July 1998): William S. Pretzer, "Reviewing Public History in Light of the *Enola Gay*" (457–61), Otto Mayr, "The *Enola Gay* Fiasco: History, Politics, and the Museum" (462–73), Pamela Walker Laird, "The Public's Historians" (474–82), and Alex Roland, "Voices in the Museum" (483–88); Robert C. Post, "A Narrative for Our Time: The *Enola Gay* 'and after that, period,'" *Technology and Culture* 45 (April 2004): 373–95; and Robert C. Post, *Who Owns America's Past? The Smithsonian and the Problem of History* (Baltimore: Johns Hopkins University Press, 2013).

20 Max Hastings, *Retribution: The Battle for Japan, 1944–45* (New York: Alfred A. Knopf, 2008), xix; Walker, "Triumph of the Middle Ground?," 99–101.

21 Charles S. Maier, *The Unmasterable Past: History, Holocaust, and German National Identity* (Cambridge: Harvard University Press, 1988), 97.

ESSAY ON SOURCES

The literature on the use of the atomic bomb is enormous. Michael Kort, Barton J. Bernstein, and J. Samuel Walker have published the most recent historiographical surveys of scholarly writing on the subject. See Kort, "The Historiography of Hiroshima: The Rise and Fall of Revisionism," *New England Journal of History* 64 (Fall 2007): 31–48; Bernstein, "Introducing the Interpretive Problems of Japan's 1945 Surrender: A Historiographical Essay on Recent Literature in the West," in *The End of the Pacific War: Reappraisals*, ed. Tsuyoshi Hasegawa (Stanford: Stanford University Press, 2007), 9–64; and Walker, "Recent Literature on Truman's Atomic Bomb Decision: The Triumph of the Middle Ground?," in *America in the World: The Historiography of American Foreign Relations since 1941*, ed. Frank Costigliola and Michael J. Hogan (New York: Cambridge University Press, 2014), 83–104 (the original version of this article appeared in *Diplomatic History* 29 [April 2005]: 311–34).

The traditional view of Truman's decision argues that he faced a choice between using the bomb and ordering an invasion of Japan that would have cost hundreds of thousands of American lives. The best book that leans heavily toward this interpretation is Wilson D. Miscamble, *The Most Controversial Decision: Truman, the Atomic Bombs, and the Defeat of Japan* (Cambridge: Cambridge University Press, 2011). For other examples, see Robert H. Ferrell, *Harry S. Truman: A Life* (Columbia: University of Missouri Press, 1994); Robert James Maddox, *Weapons for Victory: The Hiroshima Decision Fifty Years Later* (Columbia: University of

Missouri Press, 1995); Robert P. Newman, *Truman and the Hiroshima Cult* (East Lansing: Michigan State University Press, 1995); Thomas B. Allen and Norman Polmar, *Code-Name Downfall: The Secret Plan to Invade Japan and Why Truman Dropped the Bomb* (New York: Simon and Schuster, 1995); Stanley Weintraub, *The Last Great Victory: The End of World War II, July/August 1945* (New York: Dutton, 1995); D. M. Giangreco, "Casualty Projections for the U.S. Invasions of Japan, 1945–1946: Planning and Policy Implications," *Journal of Military History* 61 (July 1997): 521–82; D. M. Giangreco, "'A Score of Bloody Okinawas and Iwo Jimas': President Truman and Casualty Estimates for the Invasion of Japan," *Pacific Historical Review* 72 (February 2003): 93–132; and D. M. Giangreco, *Hell to Pay: Operation DOWNFALL and the Invasion of Japan, 1945–1947* (Annapolis: Naval Institute Press, 2009).

Revisionist scholars take sharp issue with this interpretation. They contend that the bomb was not needed to end the war and that Truman did not use it for military purposes. For examples of the revisionist view, see Ronald Takaki, *Hiroshima: Why America Dropped the Bomb* (Boston: Little, Brown, 1995); Robert Jay Lifton and Greg Mitchell, *Hiroshima in America: Fifty Years of Denial* (New York: Grosset/Putnam, 1995); Gar Alperovitz, *The Decision to Use the Atomic Bomb and the Architecture of an American Myth* (New York: Alfred A. Knopf, 1995); Dennis D. Wainstock, *The Decision to Drop the Atomic Bomb* (Westport, Conn.: Praeger, 1996); Richard H. Minear, "Atomic Holocaust, Nazi Holocaust: Some Reflections," *Diplomatic History* 19 (Spring 1995): 347–65; Philip Nobile, "On the Steps of the Smithsonian: Hiroshima Denial in America's Attic," *Judgment at the Smithsonian: The Bombing of Hiroshima and Nagasaki*, ed. Philip Nobile (New York: Marlowe, 1995); Kai Bird and Lawrence Lifschultz, "The Legend of Hiroshima," in *Hiroshima's Shadow: Writings on the Denial of History and the Smithsonian Controversy*, ed. Kai Bird and Lawrence Lifschultz (Stony Creek, Conn.: Pamphleteer's Press, 1998); Craig Collie, *Nagasaki: The Massacre of the Innocent and Unknowing* (Sydney: Allen and Unwin, 2011), and Paul Ham, *Hiroshima Nagasaki: The Real Story of the Atomic Bombings and Their Aftermath* (New York: Thomas Dunne Books, 2011).

While traditionalists and revisionists have battled over Truman's decision, other scholars have sought to move beyond fierce partisanship and evaluate the strengths and weaknesses of the opposing interpretations. The most prominent and prolific of those who take a position somewhere between the polar extremes is Barton J. Bernstein. He has produced a series of pathbreaking articles over a period of more than four decades. As new evidence has become available he has incorporated it into his scholarship, even if it required him to revise his own views. He has managed at one time or another to offend partisans on every side of the scholarly debate over the decision to use the bomb, which is a tribute to the integrity and quality of his work. See especially the following articles: "Roosevelt, Truman, and the Atomic Bomb, 1941–1945: A Reinterpretation," *Political Science*

Quarterly 90 (Spring 1975): 23–69; "The Perils and Politics of Surrender: Ending the War with Japan and Avoiding the Third Atomic Bomb," *Pacific Historical Review* 46 (February 1977): 1–26; "A Postwar Myth: 500,000 U.S. Lives Saved," *Bulletin of the Atomic Scientists* 42 (June/July 1986): 38–40; "Ike and Hiroshima: Did He Oppose It?," *Journal of Strategic Studies* 10 (September 1987): 377–89; "Compelling Japan's Surrender without the A-Bomb, Soviet Entry, or Invasion: Reconsidering the US Bombing Survey's Early-Surrender Conclusions," *Journal of Strategic Studies* 18 (June 1995): 105–48; "Eclipsed by Hiroshima and Nagasaki: Early Thinking about Tactical Nuclear Weapons," *International Security* 15 (Spring 1991): 149–73; "Writing, Righting, or Wronging the Historical Record: President Truman's Letter on His Atomic-Bomb Decision," *Diplomatic History* 16 (Winter 1992): 163–73; "Seizing the Contested Terrain of Early Nuclear History: Stimson, Conant, and Their Allies Explain the Decision to Use the Atomic Bomb," *Diplomatic History* 17 (Winter 1993): 35–72; "Understanding the Atomic Bomb and the Japanese Surrender: Missed Opportunities, Little-Known Near Disasters, and Modern Memory," *Diplomatic History* 19 (Spring 1995): 227–73; "Truman and the A-Bomb: Targeting Noncombatants, Using the Bomb, and Defending the 'Decision,'" *Journal of Military History* 62 (July 1998): 547–70; "Reconsidering Truman's Claim of 'Half a Million American Lives' Saved by the Atomic Bomb: The Construction and Deconstruction of a Myth," *Journal of Strategic Studies* 22 (March 1999): 54–95; "The Alarming Japanese Buildup on Southern Kyushu, Growing U.S. Fears, and Counterfactual Analysis: Would the Planned November 1945 Invasion of Southern Kyushu Have Occurred?," *Pacific Historical Review* 68 (November 1999): 561–609; "Reconsidering 'Invasion Most Costly': Popular-History Scholarship, Publishing Standards, and the Claim of High U.S. Casualty Estimates to Help Legitimize the Atomic Bombings," *Peace and Change* 24 (April 1999): 220–48; and "Reconsidering the 'Atomic General': Leslie R. Groves," *Journal of Military History* 67 (July 2003): 883–920.

Scholars who take a middle-ground position on the use of atomic bombs do not agree with one another on many issues. But over the past two decades, they have produced outstanding books that reject the central arguments of the traditional and revisionist interpretations. By demonstrating serious deficiencies in both, they have provided much-needed correctives to the oversimplified formulas and overheated arguments at the poles of the debate. Leading examples of excellent middle-ground scholarship include Richard B. Frank, *Downfall: The End of the Imperial Japanese Empire* (New York: Random House, 1999); Tsuyoshi Hasegawa, *Racing the Enemy: Stalin, Truman, and the Surrender of Japan* (Cambridge: Harvard University Press, 2005); Michael D. Gordin, *Five Days in August: How World War II Became a Nuclear War* (Princeton: Princeton University Press, 2007); Campbell Craig and Sergey Radchenko, *The Atomic Bomb and the Origins of the Cold War* (New Haven: Yale University Press, 2008); and Andrew J. Rotter, *Hiroshima: The World's Bomb* (Oxford: Oxford University Press, 2008).

Biographies of key figures are an important part of the literature on the use of the bomb. Two prominent biographies of Truman defend his decision. David McCullough's *Truman* (New York: Simon and Schuster, 1992) won a Pulitzer Prize and is a delight to read. Its discussion of the use of the bomb, however, is seriously flawed by complete misreadings of key documents on estimated casualty figures for an invasion of Japan and on Truman's "order" to drop the bomb. Alonzo L. Hamby's *Man of the People: A Life of Harry S. Truman* (New York: Oxford University Press, 1995) is a warmly sympathetic portrait of Truman. Hamby defends the decision to use the bomb but regrets that the United States did not make a clear statement guaranteeing the status of the emperor before Hiroshima. Arnold A. Offner, *Another Such Victory: President Truman and the Cold War, 1945–1953* (Stanford: Stanford University Press, 2003), by contrast, sharply criticizes Truman and accepts much, but not all, of the revisionist position.

Biographies of other prominent figures are valuable resources for studying the decision to use the bomb. I have found the following especially useful: Robert L. Messer, *The End of an Alliance: James F. Byrnes, Roosevelt, Truman, and the Origins of the Cold War* (Chapel Hill: University of North Carolina Press, 1982); David Robertson, *Sly and Able: A Political Biography of James F. Byrnes* (New York: W. W. Norton, 1994); James G. Hershberg, *James B. Conant: Harvard to Hiroshima and the Making of the Nuclear Age* (New York: Alfred A. Knopf, 1993); Kai Bird, *The Chairman: John J. McCloy and the Making of the American Establishment* (New York: Simon and Schuster, 1992); Forrest C. Pogue, *George C. Marshall: Statesman* (New York: Viking, 1987); Mark A. Stoler, *George C. Marshall: Soldier-Statesman of the American Century* (Boston: Twayne, 1989); William Lanouette with Bela Silard, *Genius in the Shadows: A Biography of Leo Szilard, the Man behind the Bomb* (New York: Scribner's, 1992); and Robert S. Norris, *Racing for the Bomb: General Leslie R. Groves, the Manhattan Project's Indispensable Man* (South Royalton, Vt.: Steerforth Press, 2002). Herbert Bix was awarded the Pulitzer Prize for *Hirohito and the Making of Modern Japan* (New York: HarperCollins, 2000). Kai Bird and Martin J. Sherwin received a Pulitzer for their biography *American Prometheus: The Triumph and Tragedy of J. Robert Oppenheimer* (New York: Alfred A. Knopf, 2005).

In addition to those listed above, several other noteworthy articles should be consulted by students of the decision to use the bomb: Michael J. Yavenditti, "The American People and the Use of Atomic Bombs on Japan," *Historian* 36 (February 1974): 224–47; Robert L. Messer, "New Evidence on Truman's Decision," *Bulletin of the Atomic Scientists* 41 (August 1985): 50–56; Rufus E. Miles Jr., "Hiroshima: The Strange Myth of Half a Million American Lives Saved," *International Security* 10 (Fall 1985): 121–40; Marc Gallicchio, "After Nagasaki: General Marshall's Plan for Tactical Nuclear Weapons in Japan," *Prologue* 23 (Winter 1991): 396–404; William Lanouette, "Why We Dropped the Bomb," *Civilization* 2 (January–February 1995): 28–39; Peter Maslowski, "Truman, the Bomb, and the Numbers Game," *MHQ: The Quarterly Journal of Military History* 7 (Spring 1995): 103–7; Stanley

Goldberg, "Racing to the Finish: The Decision to Bomb Hiroshima and Naga-saki," *Journal of American–East Asian Relations* 4 (Summer 1995): 117–28; Melvyn P. Leffler, "Truman's Decision to Drop the Atomic Bomb," *IHJ Bulletin* 15 (Summer 1995): 1–7; Donald Kagan, "Why America Dropped the Bomb," *Commentary* 100 (September 1995): 17–23; Robert A. Pape, "Why Japan Surrendered," *International Security* 18 (Fall 1993): 154–201; Robert P. Newman, "Hiroshima and the Trashing of Henry Stimson," *New England Quarterly* 71 (March 1998): 5–32; Ward Wilson, "The Winning Weapon? Rethinking Nuclear Weapons in Light of Hiroshima," *International Security* 31 (Spring 2007): 162–79; Sean L. Malloy, "'A Very Pleasant Way to Die': Radiation Effects and the Decision to Use the Atomic Bomb against Japan," *Diplomatic History* 36 (June 2012): 515–45; and Richard B. Frank, "Ketsu Go, Downfall, and Ending the War: Japanese and American Political and Military Strategy in 1945," forthcoming in *Nuclear Energy and the Legacy of Harry S. Truman*, ed. J. Samuel Walker (Kirksville, Mo.: Truman State University Press, 2016).

The politics and deliberations of the Japanese government over ending the war are a vital part of the events that led to Hiroshima, and several historians have made good use of records that have opened since the death of Hirohito in 1989. In addition to the works of Richard Frank, Tsuyoshi Hasegawa, and Herbert P. Bix cited above, see Sadao Asada, "The Shock of the Atomic Bomb and Japan's Decision to Surrender—a Reconsideration," *Pacific Historical Review* 67 (November 1998): 477–512; Herbert P. Bix, "Japan's Delayed Surrender: A Reinterpretation," *Diplomatic History* 19 (Spring 1995): 197–225; articles by Frank, Hasegawa, and Sumio Hatano in Hasegawa, ed., *The End of the Pacific War*; and Yukiko Koshiro, *Imperial Eclipse: Japan's Strategic Thinking about Continental Asia before August 1945* (Ithaca: Cornell University Press, 2013). Edward J. Drea, *In the Service of the Emperor: Essays on the Imperial Japanese Army* (Lincoln: University of Nebraska Press, 1998) is an important collection that supports the views of Asada, Frank, Hasegawa, and Bix that Hirohito had not decided on surrender before Hiroshima.

The best sources for the Soviet side of the diplomatic aspects of the atomic bomb are Hasegawa, *Racing the Enemy*, and David Holloway, *Stalin and the Bomb: The Soviet Union and the Arms Race, 1939–1956* (New Haven: Yale University Press, 1994), which draw on documents released after the demise of the Soviet Union. See also the essays by Hasegawa and Holloway in Hasegawa, ed., *The End of the Pacific War*. Richard Rhodes's *Dark Sun: The Making of the Hydrogen Bomb* (New York: Simon and Schuster, 1995) adds valuable information on Soviet espionage.

The volume of the literature on subjects closely related to the use of the bomb—the Manhattan Project, the Pacific War, and strategic bombing—is stag-gering. The works that I have found most useful on those subjects are cited in the chapter notes.

Students of Truman's use of atomic bombs are fortunate to have an abun-dance of primary evidence easily available in published form. Michael B. Stoff,

Jonathan F. Fanton, and R. Hal Williams, editors of *The Manhattan Project: A Documentary Introduction to the Atomic Age* (Philadelphia: Temple University Press, 1991), provide facsimiles of a wide range of key documents from the records of the Manhattan Project, the papers of Franklin D. Roosevelt and Henry L. Stimson, and other sources. Dennis Merrill, editor of *Documentary History of the Truman Presidency, Volume 1: The Decision to Drop the Atomic Bomb on Japan* (Bethesda, Md.: University Publications of America, 1995), performs the same service for a rich variety of records and papers from the Harry S. Truman Library in Independence, Missouri. Robert H. Ferrell has edited Truman's Potsdam diary notes in *Off the Record: The Private Papers of Harry S. Truman* (New York: Harper and Row, 1980) and his letters to his wife in *Dear Bess: The Letters from Harry to Bess Truman, 1910–1959* (New York: W. W. Norton, 1983). William Burr of the National Security Archive has compiled a splendid set of documents relating to the bomb and the end of the war. See "The Atomic Bomb and the End of World War II: A Collection of Primary Sources," available at http://www.gwu .edu/~nsarchiv/NSAEBB/NSAEBB162/.

This book draws on the work of the scholars listed above, but it also draws on research in unpublished primary evidence that I consulted in attempts to resolve disputed historiographical issues and seek new insights on a complex subject. The documentary sources that I found most helpful were the Harry S. Truman Papers at the Truman Library; the George C. Marshall Papers at the George C. Marshall Foundation Research Library and Museum at the Virginia Military Institute in Lexington, Virginia; the papers of James F. Byrnes at Clemson University in Clemson, South Carolina; the papers of William D. Leahy, Joseph E. Davies, Edward L. Bowles, and H. H. Arnold at the Library of Congress in Washington, D.C.; and the records of the Office of the Secretary of War (Record Group 107), the U.S. Joint Chiefs of Staff (Record Group 218), and the War Department General and Special Staffs (Record Group 165) at the National Archives in College Park, Maryland.

INDEX

Bard, Ralph A., 14, 42, 90
Bataan Death March, 21
Bernstein, Barton J., 60, 94, 103,
    115–16 (n. 12), 124 (n. 25)
Bix, Herbert P., 123 (n. 12)
Bock's Car, 76–77
Bombing Strategy (U.S.): evolution
    of, 24–28, 95; Marshall's doubts
    about, 34, 37–39; projected as cause
    for Japanese surrender, 38
Bundy, Harvey A., 100
Bundy, McGeorge, 100–101, 127
    (n. 10)
Burns, James MacGregor, 10
Bush, Vannevar, 14
Byrnes, James F.: background, 3–4;
    and postwar casualty estimates, 4,
    102; informs Truman about bomb,
    13; as member of Interim Commit-
    tee, 14, 17; and diplomatic advan-
    tages of bomb, 17–18, 62–65, 71, 94;
    and unconditional surrender, 45,
    68; and demonstration of bomb,
    51; and Potsdam Conference, 52,
    55, 58; and Soviet Union, 62–65,
    94; and Potsdam Proclamation, 68;
    and Japanese peace overture, 84–86

Caron, Robert, 74
Casualties: postwar estimates of, 2–5,
    96, 101–3, 107–8, 128–29 (n. 10);
    wartime estimates of, 5, 34–38,
    92–94, 114 (n. 4); Truman's com-
    mitment to minimizing, 9–10, 34,
    70, 92–94; in island campaign, 23; at
    Iwo Jima, 23; in battle of Okinawa,
    30–31; suffered by U.S. in July 1945,
    70, 92; projections of if war contin-
    ued, 92–94; scholarly views of, 107,
    114–16 (n. 12)
Cate, James L., 101
Cavert, Samuel McCrea, 96
Child, Marquis, 9
Churchill, Winston S., 1, 15, 18, 52,
    53; and casualty estimates, 3, 102;

and Yalta agreement, 15; Truman's
    comments on, 52, 119 (n. 7); and
    Potsdam Conference, 52–53, 57,
    60–61, 65
Compton, Karl T., 14
Conant, James B.: as member of
    Interim Committee, 14; recom-
    mends target for bomb, 15, 99; and
    criticism of use of bomb, 99–100,
    127 (n. 8)
Cousins, Norman, 98

Davies, Joseph E., 62
Doolittle, Jimmy, 21
Dower, John W., 20, 21, 113 (n. 1)
Drea, Edward J., 115 (n. 12)
Dulles, Allen, 47

Eaker, Ira C., 34, 38, 90
Eichelberger, Robert, 91
Einstein, Albert, 10, 17
Eisenhower, Dwight D., 90
Enola Gay, 74, 76, 104–6

Farrell, Thomas F., 57–58
Federal Council of Churches, 96
Feis, Herbert, 90, 102–3
Fermi, Enrico, 11
Ferrell, Robert H., 115 (n. 12)
Finletter, Thomas K., 98
Forrestal, James V., 34, 42, 67, 84, 85,
    90
Franck, James, 118–19 (n. 38)
Frank, Richard B., 88, 124 (n. 23)

Gallup poll, 4–5, 44, 84, 98
Giangreco, D. M., 115–16 (n. 12)
Goldberg, Stanley, 112 (n. 7)
Gosling, F. G., 112 (n. 8)
Grew, Joseph C.: concerns about
    Soviet Union, 40; and uncondi-
    tional surrender, 41–42, 46, 67
Groves, Leslie R.: personality of,
    11–12; consultation with Interim
    Committee, 14; projections for

completion of bomb, 14, 17, 18, 49; and Trinity test, 53–55, 57–59, 61; and bombing of Kyoto, 59; and order to use bomb, 59; justification of Manhattan Project, 94; and post-war casualty estimates, 102

Ham, Paul, 79
Hamby, Alonzo L., 8
Handy, Thomas T., 59, 66, 91
Hansell, Haywood S., Jr., 25
Harper's Magazine, 100–101, 102
Harrison, George L., 14, 55
Hasegawa, Tsuyoshi, 124 (n. 25)
Hersey, John, 98
Hewlett, Richard G., 112 (n. 8)
Heyman, I. Michael, 105
Hirohito (emperor): status of, 29–30, 41; ambivalence about ending war, 30, 48; American attitudes toward, 44; role in ending war, 81–83, 86–89; response to atomic bomb, 82–86; concern about popular discontent, 83, 89; radio broadcast by, 86–87
Hopkins, Harry, 16, 39, 63

Indianapolis, USS, 70–71, 74, 93
Interim Committee: membership of, 14; deliberations of, 14–15, 16–18; and targeting of atomic bomb, 14–15, 49, 99; considers impact of bomb on U.S.-Soviet relations, 16–17, 60; considers demonstration of bomb, 49; and Franck report, 118–19 (n. 38)
Invasion of Japan (U.S.): postwar casualty estimates for, 2–5, 96, 101–3, 107–8, 115–16 (n. 12); atomic bomb as alternative to, 4–5, 48–49, 101–9 ; wartime casualty projections for, 5, 34–37, 92–94, 114 (n. 4); authorized by Truman, 34, 35, 48; necessity of for ending war, 34–36, 87–92, 94, 96, 102–3, 126 (n. 4);

Strategic Bombing Survey on, 98–99
Invasion of Manchuria (by Soviet Union): U.S. desire for, 16, 35, 39–40, 56–57; as alternative to U.S. invasion, 39–40, 87–88; re-vised U.S. view on, 62–64; Stalin's eagerness for, 64–65; effect of on Japan, 80–83, 87–89, 96; Strategic Bombing Survey on, 98–99; Army Intelligence report discusses, 126 (n. 4)
Irokawa, Daikichi, 29
Iwo Jima, 22, 23, 74

Japan: weakness of, 5, 27–30, 36, 89, 91; atrocities committed by, 21, 24; conduct of war by, 21–23, 29; and revival of imperialism, 44, 84; and approach to Soviet Union, 30, 45–47; "peace feelers" of, 47; and end of war, 69–70, 80–89. *See also* Hirohito; Supreme Council for the Direction of the War
Johnson, Lyndon B., 100
Joint Chiefs of Staff (U.S.), and casualty estimates, 34–37; views on ending war, 34–38, 39–40; and unconditional surrender, 41, 67; concern about public morale, 39; and sudden end of war, 66–67
Joint Intelligence Committee (U.S.), 38
Joint War Plans Committee (U.S.), 36–37, 116 (n. 12)

Kaltenborn, H. V., 80
Kennedy, John F., 100
Kido, Kōichi, 29, 30, 43, 81, 82, 83, 86
King, Ernest J., 34, 39, 40, 90

Leahy, William D.: role of in White House meeting, 34; and uncon-ditional surrender, 35, 42, 67, 84, 85; and casualty estimates, 35,

Sherwin, Martin J., 103
Skates, John Ray, 115 (n. 12)
Smithsonian Institution, 104–6
Soong, T. V., 63
Soviet Union. *See* Invasion of
    Manchuria; Stalin, Joseph
Spaatz, Carl A., 59, 90
Special Committee to Investigate the
    National Defense Program, 13
Stalin, Joseph, 1, 17, 49, 52, 119 (n. 1);
    and Yalta agreement, 15; and entry
    into Pacific War, 16, 39, 53, 55–57,
    62–66, 80; favors early summit, 18,
    53; meets Truman at Potsdam, 52,
    55–57, 91; Truman's views of, 56,
    64; and Potsdam negotiations, 57,
    60–61; and atomic bomb, 64–65, 80,
    121 (n. 29)
Stimson, Henry L., background, 2;
    and postwar casualty estimates, 2,
    100–101, 107; postwar explanations
    for use of bomb, 3, 94, 100–103; in-
    forms Truman about bomb, 13–14;
    and Interim Committee, 14, 15; at
    June 18 White House meeting, 34,
    35; and unconditional surrender,
    42, 67; discussion of war's end with
    Marshall, 48–49; informs Truman
    about atomic test, 55, 57; approval
    of order to use bomb, 59; and
    targets for atomic bomb, 59; and
    diplomatic uses of bomb, 60–62;
    and Soviet entry into war, 63; and
    Japanese peace overture, 84, 85; re-
    ports to Truman on Hiroshima, 85;
    article about use of bomb, 100–101,
    127 (n. 10)
Strategic Bombing Survey, U.S.,
    77–79, 98–99, 103
Supreme Council for the Direction
    of the War: and concerns about na-
    tional polity, 29, 30, 81–86; internal
    divisions over ending war, 29, 43,
    45–47, 69, 81–86; and unconditional
    surrender, 43

Suzuki, Kantarō, 28, 29, 67–70, 81,
    82, 86
Sweeney, Charles W., 76
Szilard, Leo, 17, 118 (n. 38)

Tibbets, Paul W., 74
Tōgō, Shigenori, seeks end of war, 29,
    80–83, 86; exchanges cables with
    Satō, 45–47; and Zacharias broad-
    cast, 68; and Potsdam Declaration,
    69
Toyoda, Soemu, 29, 82, 83
Trinity atomic test, description of,
    53–55, 57–58; as boost to Truman's
    confidence, 57, 60–61; and diplo-
    matic uses of bomb, 62–65
Truman, Bess Wallace, 10, 52, 57, 62,
    64, 103
Truman, Harry S., comments on
    Byrnes, 4; casualty estimates cited
    by after war, 4–5, 92–93, 101–2,
    108; choice between invasion and
    use of bomb, 5, 89–93, 101–6, 108;
    personality, 8; problems faced
    on becoming president, 8–9; and
    Roosevelt's legacy, 9–10, 118 (n. 31);
    commitment to minimizing casual-
    ties, 10, 34, 70–71, 92–93; World
    War I experience, 10, 70; establish-
    ment of Interim Committee, 14;
    and U.S.-Soviet relations, 15–16, 35,
    56, 60–65, 94–95; and diplomatic
    advantages of bomb, 18, 52–53,
    62–64, 71, 94–95; and Potsdam
    Conference, 18, 34, 52–62; and
    unconditional surrender, 35, 41–42,
    44–45, 48, 68, 71, 84–85, 117 (n. 31);
    approval of invasion of Kyushu,
    35, 48; and Soviet entry into war,
    40, 56–57, 60, 62–64; and military
    advantages of atomic bomb, 48, 58,
    71, 92–93; comments on Churchill,
    52, 119 (n. 7); and timing of atomic
    test, 53–54; reaction to Trinity
    test, 55, 56–58, 60–62; comments

on Stalin, 56, 64; reasons for using atomic bomb, 58, 92–96, 101–7, 125 (n. 33); and consideration of using bomb, 58, 101–2, 127 (n. 10); and order to drop bomb, 59, 120 (n. 15); and targets for atomic bomb, 59–60; telling of Stalin about bomb, 64–65; response to Hiroshima, 76, 80, 85; and Japanese peace overture, 83–85; orders no further atomic attacks, 85, 95; limited knowledge of situation in Japan, 91, 92, 93; casualty estimates cited by during war, 92–93, 114–16 (n. 12); requesting of bomb study, 98; diary of discovered, 103

Umezu, Yoshijiro, 29, 82, 83
Unconditional surrender: support for modifying, 35, 40–43, 45; Truman's attitude toward, 35, 41–42, 44–45, 48, 68, 71, 84–85, 117 (n. 31); modification of as alternative to invasion, 40–47; origins of policy, 41; as impediment to ending war, 41–42, 48, 68; potential drawbacks of modifying, 43–44, 48; popularity

of, 44, 84, 117–18 (n. 31); Army intelligence view of Japanese message on, 46; and Potsdam Declaration, 68–69; and Japanese peace overture, 83–85

Vinson, Fred M., 39, 66

Wallace, Henry A., 3, 9, 85
Wall Street Journal, 105
War, alternatives for ending: Truman asks for Joint Chiefs' judgment on, 34; advantages and drawbacks of, 37–58, 95; advantages of atomic bomb, 48, 58–59, 92–96; Strategic Bombing Survey on, 98–99; in Stimson's article, 100–101; discussed by scholars, 102–8. *See also* Bombing strategy; Invasion of Japan; Invasion of Manchuria; Unconditional surrender
Weckerling, John, 46

Yalta conference, 15–16, 39, 63, 65
Yonai, Mitsumasa, 29, 82, 87

Zacharias, Ellis M., 68